NEW MERMAIDS

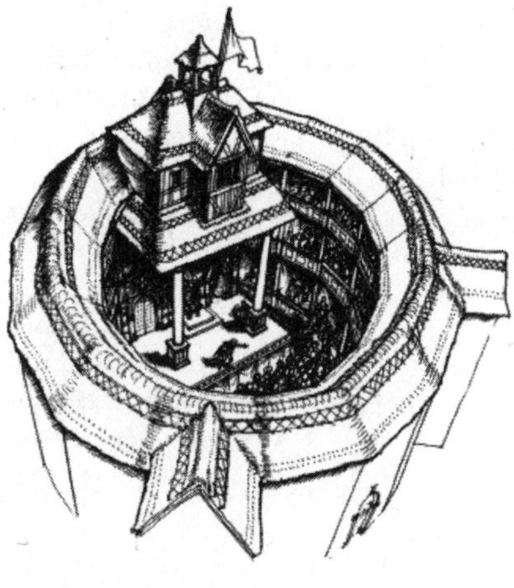

Reconstruction of an Elizabethan Theatre
by C. Walter Hodges

NEW MERMAIDS

The Alchemist
All for Love
Arden of Faversham
Arms and the Man
Bartholmew Fair
The Beaux' Stratagem
The Beggar's Opera
The Changeling
A Chaste Maid in Cheapside
The Country Wife
The Critic
Doctor Faustus
The Duchess of Malfi
The Dutch Courtesan
Eastward Ho!
Edward the Second
Elizabethan and Jacobean Tragedies
Epicoene, or The Silent Woman
Every Man In His Humour
Gammer Gurton's Needle
An Ideal Husband
The Importance of Being Earnest
The Jew of Malta
The Knight of the Burning Pestle
Lady Windermere's Fan
London Assurance
Love for Love
Major Barbara
The Malcontent
The Man of Mode
Marriage A-La-Mode
Mrs Warren's Profession
A New Way to Pay Old Debts
The Old Wife's Tale
The Playboy of the Western World
The Provoked Wife
Pygmalion
The Recruiting Officer
The Relapse
The Revenger's Tragedy
The Rivals
The Roaring Girl
The Rover
Saint Joan
The School for Scandal
She Stoops to Conquer
The Shoemaker's Holiday
The Spanish Tragedy
Tamburlaine
The Tamer Tamed
Three Late Medieval Morality Plays
  Mankind
  Everyman
  Mundus et Infans
'Tis Pity She's a Whore
The Tragedy of Mariam
Volpone
The Way of the World
The White Devil
The Witch
The Witch of Edmonton
A Woman Killed with Kindness
A Woman of No Importance
Women Beware Women

NEW MERMAIDS

APHRA BEHN

THE ROVER

Edited by Robyn Bolam
Professor Emeritus, St Mary's University College,
Twickenham

Methuen Drama India
An imprint of Bloomsbury Publishing Plc

BLOOMSBURY
NEW DELHI • LONDON • OXFORD • NEW YORK • SYDNEY

BLOOMSBURY INDIA
Bloomsbury Publishing India Pvt. Ltd
Second Floor, LSC Building No. 4, DDA Complex, Pocket C–6&7,
Vasant Kunj, New Delhi 110070

BLOOMSBURY, Bloomsbury Methuen Drama India and the Diana logo are trademarks of Bloomsbury Publishing Plc

First published in India 2021
First published 2012 by Bloomsbury Publishing Plc
Reprinted 2013
Reprinted by Bloomsbury Methuen Drama 2014 (twice), 2015, 2016, 2017, 2018, 2019 (twice), 2021 (twice)

For legal purposes the Acknowledgements on p. vi constitute an extension of this copyright page.

This edition published with permission from Bloomsbury Publishing Plc,
50 Bedford Square, London, WC1B3DP, UK

British Library Cataloguing-in-Publication Data
A catalogue record for this book is available from the British Library.

Library of Congress Cataloging-in-Publication Data
A catalog record for this book is available from the Library of Congress

ISBN: 978-93-54351-89-1

10 9 8 7 6 5 4 3 2 1
For sale in the Indian subcontinent only

Series: New Mermaids
Printed and bound in India by Sanat Printers

CONTENTS

ACKNOWLEDGEMENTS

I am indebted to all past and present editors of *The Rover*, particularly Frederick M. Link and Janet Todd, and to the many directors and theatre companies who have responded so imaginatively to the play's challenges. Particular thanks go to Joss Costello for making a recording of his original production available to me. Many of the texts listed in 'Further Reading' also proved invaluable. I would like to thank the staff of the British Library and I am extremely grateful to Professor Brian Gibbons for his help and guidance throughout the preparation of this volume.

INTRODUCTION

About the Play

The most popular of Aphra Behn's plays, *The Rover* has all the stock ingredients of Restoration drama – an attractive libertine, a spirited heroine, a domineering quasi-parental figure to be thwarted, and a foolish but endearing fop, trying unsuccessfully to be a rake. Florinda and Belvile's love-match, opposed by family and rival suitors, belongs to an old dramatic tradition, as does Callis's role of the governess or nurse. Angellica Bianca moves beyond the traditional stereotype of a prostitute to become a complex version of the dangerous scorned mistress. Yet, for all these recognisable characteristics and the incorporation of songs, music, sword-play, and dancing which an audience might expect from a play of this period, *The Rover* is full of surprises. On the surface, Behn appears to be working within the literary conventions of her day, but under it she pushes their boundaries as far as she dares.

The play is set in the 1650s, a period which must have seemed, to English Royalists, like an indefinite extension of Lent, with the suppression of pastimes and sports by Cromwell's Protectorate. Exiled in Naples, cavaliers make merry in a carnival setting, associated with Roman Saturnalian revels as well as with opposition to the restrictions of the Christian tradition's Lent, which included a ban on sexual intercourse as well as the eating of meat. It is a time of misrule; everything is turned upside down, prohibitions are temporarily removed, and privileges and rank suspended. Carnival may have appealed to Restoration audiences because of its emphasis on sexual freedom, and to Behn because it extended this freedom to women as well as men. Her female characters often take the initiative and she has been credited with creating more daring dialogue between the sexes than many of her male contemporaries. In *The Rover*, she uses this successfully to explore issues of love and fidelity, trickery and deception, male power, forced marriage, prostitution, and what it means to be an outsider.

Behn is skilled in complex staging techniques. The pace is often fast and the action hectic, with disguises and asides producing both comic effect and tension. The play's structure sets up many thought-provoking moments: Jacqueline Pearson draws attention to the way Behn mirrors the behaviour and experiences of Belvile and Florinda in I.ii and IV.ii and, again, in IV.i and IV.iii, which 'emphasizes the equality between the lovers'.[1] Culminating in a love-match between a convent girl and a pirate, *The Rover* remains a performable, entertaining play because of its insights into relationships between the sexes and its opportunities for female wit, spectacle, swashbuckling comedy, rapid dramatic transitions, and the creation of intimacy between players and spectators in a wide variety of theatrical settings.

The Author

Aphra Behn was probably born in 1640,[2] a year of political crisis during which Charles I's eleven years of personal rule ended, the theatres were closed, and civil war became inevitable. The king was beheaded in 1649 and Behn grew up during the Commonwealth years, coming of age just after the Restoration of Charles II in 1660 and the reopening of the theatres. Having lived through the reigns of Charles and his brother, who became James II, she died on 16 April 1689,[3] two months into the reign of William III and James's daughter, Mary.

The few recorded details of her life are sometimes contradictory and errors have caused further confusion.[4] Her parents were, most likely, Bartholomew Johnson, a Canterbury barber, and his wife Elizabeth (née Denham): an Aphra Johnson was baptised at Harbledown, near Canterbury, on 14 December 1640. Behn's knowledge of languages and her writing ability suggested to many biographers that she had received an education and must, therefore, have been of a higher social station than the daughter of a barber. Perhaps even the first biographical piece, *The Life and Memoirs . . . by One of the Fair Sex*, published in 1696 and written not long after Behn's death as a preface to her collected fictional works, made such an assumption.[5] However, a note by Anne, Countess of Winchelsea, who lived locally and might, according to Jane Jones, be expected to know if Behn was not, as *The Life and Memoirs* stated, 'a

1 Jacqueline Pearson, 'Women Spectators, Playwrights, and Performers on the Restoration Stage' in *Teaching British Women Playwrights of the Restoration and Eighteenth Century*, eds. Bonnie Nelson & Catherine Burroughs, New York, 2010, p. 56.

2 Most critics now agree, although Sara Heller Mendelson argues for a date at the end of the 1640s (*The Mental World of Stuart Women*, Brighton, 1987, p. 116) and Janet Todd also raises the possibility of a date after 1640 (T, p. 2).

3 *The Life and Memoirs...by One of the Fair Sex*, in Aphra Behn, *The Histories and Novels of the Late Ingenious Mrs Behn*, London, 1696 (B.L. Catalogue no. C.57 K.24) gives 1686 as the date of Behn's death. Thomas Culpepper (Colepeper) states 1689 in his *Adversaria* (B.L. Harley MS 7588, sig.426 v. and sig.453 v.), but differs on the day, giving 16 and 29 April, respectively.

4 In *The Dictionary of National Bibliography*, Edmund Gosse lists an Aphra Johnson, baptised on 10 July 1640. This has since been shown to be an Aphra Amis, who was buried two days later. See Jane Jones, 'New light on the background and early life of Aphra Behn' in *Notes and Queries* 235 (1990), 289.

5 See note 3 above.

gentlewoman by birth', records that she was 'Daughter to a Barber . . . though the account of her life before her Works pretends otherwise'.[6] Jones comments that this information also accords with a number of contemporary documents relating to Bartholomew Johnson.

Behn's mother appears to have had higher social connections, despite her inability or disinclination to sign her name on her marriage allegation in 1638.[7] Jones believes that Elizabeth Denham had a brother who attended university and eventually became a doctor,[8] and that she may have traded the higher social status due to her by birth for a more humble, married respectability after the couple's first child, Frances, was conceived. In Thomas Colepeper's *Adversaria*, probably written shortly after Behn's death, it is noted that:

> Mrs Been was born at Stürrey or Canterbury, her name was Johnson, so that she might be called Ben Johnson, she had also a fayer sister maryed to Capt. Write, their Names were ffranck, & Aphora, was Mr. Beene.[9]

Earlier in the manuscript Behn is called, 'foster sister to the Colonell, her mother being the Colonell's nurse' who 'gave him suck for some time'. It is now assumed that the writer was Sir Thomas Culpepper, an orphan from the age of five, and that he and 'the Colonell' were the same person. The description of Behn as a 'foster sister' to Sir Thomas might be no more than an expression of their closeness as children: his affection for and admiration of her is apparent. If she was treated as one of the family she would also have enjoyed certain privileges not usually accorded to a barber's daughter and these may explain her education. Canterbury's proximity to the continent would also have given Behn daily opportunities to hear several European languages: Jones notes the abundance of 'French-speaking Huguenot refugees' in the city and the 'large Dutch Congregation' in 'nearby Sandwich'.[10]

In 1663, at the age of 23, Behn travelled with her family on the appointment of her father as Lieutenant-General of the English colony of

6 *The Poems of Anne Countess of Winchilsea: from the original ed. of 1713 and from unpublished ms*, ed. M. Reynolds, (Decennial Publications Series 2, vol.5) Chicago, 1903, p. 427. B.L. Catalogue no. AC2691d/11.

7 Canterbury Cathedral Library, uncatalogued.

8 See Jones, op. cit., 290.

9 See note 3 above. Culpepper was born in 1637 and the Johnsons' first child was baptised on 6 December 1638, so it is conceivable that Elizabeth Johnson was his wet nurse for a time.

10 See Jones, op. cit., 291.

Surinam and thirty six other islands. Jones suggests that this unlikely occurrence may have been a result of Bartholomew Johnson's and his daughter's involvement in pro-Royalist activities during the 1659 attempt to restore the king,[11] but no evidence for this has been found. Behn's father apparently died on the journey and, after approximately two months in Surinam, the family left. Shortly afterwards, Aphra Johnson became Aphra Behn. She may have married a London merchant of 'Dutch extraction', as the *Life and Memoirs* states, or the German ('ffranck') Johan Behn, who sailed in the West Indies, possibly on the boat which brought the Johnsons back from Surinam, as Jones plausibly argues – or it might be that, as a prelude to earning an independent living in the theatre, Aphra looked for inspiration to a great dramatist, who died three years before she was born – adding the 'h' in her maiden name to his fore-name, and wittily making herself 'Behn Johnson'.[12]

No marriage records for Behn exist and she never refers to a husband: the man most documented in her life was John Hoyle, a bisexual lawyer. Whether she experienced an arranged marriage with an elderly man who died of plague shortly after, whether she married a younger Able Seaman on impulse and quickly separated, or whether she remained unmarried throughout her life, is still unproven. We know that Thomas Killigrew recruited her to spy for Charles II in the Dutch wars of 1666, but she remained unpaid and was threatened with – if not actually subjected to – incarceration in a debtors' prison in 1668, her pleas to Killigrew and the king apparently having been ignored. Perhaps as a result of this treatment, although she had presented an Indian costume to Killigrew's King's Company on her return from Surinam, her plays were performed by the rival Duke's Company from 1670. Between 1670 and 1689 she produced 18 plays, being the most prolific playwright of her day, second only to Dryden.

Aphra Behn was the first female professional writer in England. She inspired budding writers, both male and female, and was a poet and editor of miscellanies, a pioneer of the short novel (most famously, *Oroonoko*, in 1688), a writer of short stories, and a translator of texts in several languages. Subject to literary misogyny, slandered as well as praised in her own time and since, Behn's work is finally being appreciated as it deserves.

11 Ibid., 292.

12 Thomas Culpepper remarked on the combination of names and Mary Ann O'Donnell also makes this suggestion ('Tory wit and unconventional woman: Aphra Behn' in *Women Writers of the Seventeenth Century*, eds. Katharina M. Wilson & Frank J. Warnke, Athens, Ga., 1989, p. 352).

Although her family may have been Protestant (her father was made Overseer of the Poor for St Margaret's Parish in Canterbury in 1654),[13] there are several indications that, by the end of her life, Behn was a Catholic;[14] yet, in the new Protestant reign, she was given the rare privilege of a burial in the cloisters of Westminster Abbey on 20 April 1689. Her black marble slab is inscribed:

> Here lies a proof that wit can never be
> Defence enough against mortality.[15]

Perhaps not, but the wit of the woman known as Astrea has proved an admirable defence against many other things, ensuring her continued popularity.

The Play

From Page to Stage

The Rover was first performed and the play text published in 1677 (licensed July 2nd). Copies of three issues of the first Quarto still exist, exhibiting minor differences. Although she was the acknowledged author of at least four plays by the time she wrote *The Rover*, Behn or her publisher chose to bring out its first issue and most of its second, anonymously. Only towards the end of the second issue's printing run was the phrase, 'especially of our sex' inserted after 'dominion' at line 21 of the postscript – a hint that she was no longer attempting to conceal her identity – and the title-page of the third issue gave her name: Mrs. A. Behn.

The postscript, only printed in the first Quarto, acknowledges occasional similarities with Richard Brome's *The Novella* (1632),[16] but Behn's main source for *The Rover* was a lengthy closet drama by Thomas Killigrew, *Thomaso, or The Wanderer*, which was written in 1654,[17] and may never have been acted. Unusually for her, Behn borrowed substantially from Killigrew (appropriating large sections of dialogue word for word), and the opening of her postscript suggests that this was probably the reason why *The Rover* did not bear its author's name from the outset. However, she was not a plagiarist in the usual sense, which becomes

13 Canterbury Cathedral Library J/Q/453i. See Jones, op. cit., 293.

14 See Gerald Duchovnay, 'Aphra Behn's religion', *Notes and Queries* 221 (1976), 235–7.

15 Reproduced in Thomas Culpepper's *Adversaria*, sig.426 r.

16 See Frederick M. Link, ed., *The Rover* (Regent's Restoration Drama Series), Lincoln, Nebraska & London, 1967, p. 130.

17 *Thomaso* was printed in London in 1663 in Killigrew's *Comedies and Tragedies* (B.L. Catalogue no. C.39. K.4.).

clearer if we focus on her innovations and changes, rather than on basic similarities. When she retained the names of Killigrew's characters, as in the case of Angellica Bianca, Behn often altered their personalities and actions so that they are presented as new creations, and Killigrew's dialogue may occasionally be reproduced, e.g. at I.i.114–18, but when assigned to a new character (particularly one of a different sex), and rearranged, the force of its impact is increased. She was adept at creating moments of dramatic tension and, by condensing, cutting, refocusing, and making important additions to Killigrew's text, she quickened its pace considerably and made it into a successful and performable drama.[18] Behn invented Valeria and paired her with Frederick; she split Killigrew's Thomaso into two – his wanderer element lives on in Willmore, while his faithful qualities are developed in a new character, Belvile. Hellena is Behn's invention although, surprisingly, she borrowed from Killigrew's Harrigo ('a sober English gentleman') and even from *Thomaso*'s so-called 'good courtesans', Angellica and Paulina, for some of her speeches and, in the case of the latter, part of her background. Blunt, who is closely based on Killigrew's Edwardo, came to life when Behn redefined his role in relation to the main plot and associated him with the catch-phrase, ''adsheartlikins'.

While Killigrew modelled Thomaso on himself, as the name suggests, Behn probably incorporated elements of John Wilmot, Earl of Rochester into Willmore. Both Behn and Elizabeth Barry, who initially played the part of Hellena, knew Rochester. Although Willmore only engages in single-sex promiscuity, for the creation of his character Behn may also have drawn on her own relationship with John Hoyle. The most famous rover of them all was Charles II who, according to 'Tory mythology . . . on the verge of fleeing England, disguised himself in buff'[19] – so not only Willmore's libertinism, but even his costume is linked to the 'Prince' he serves in the play.

Behn strengthened both character and plot by cutting Angellica Bianca's involvement in the action. Killigrew's Angellica regards herself as a victim and remains in love with Thomaso at the close: she is not allowed to control her fate, being ignorant of the arrangement by which Thomaso and Don Pedro agree to dispose of her. Behn's character refuses to see herself as being morally inferior and attempts to make her own

18 See also J. De Ritter, 'The gypsy, the rover, and the wanderer: Aphra Behn's revision of Thomas Killigrew', *Restoration: Studies in English Literary Culture 1600–1700*, 10 (1986), 82–92.

19 Susan Staves, *Players' Scepters: Fictions of Authority in the Restoration*, Lincoln, Nebraska, 1979, p. 2.

decisions. Behn also gave her the power to hold Willmore at pistol-point, finally sparing his life. Killigrew created characters through whom he advocated female emancipation (such as Harrigo), but Behn tackled the issue more thoroughly Above all, the biggest difference in these two plays is one of liveliness of atmosphere, rather than specific characters or instances: Behn produced a drama in which the spirit of carnival is paramount.

Carnival

In carnival, everyone, however different, can be integrated by joining in. As Mikhail Bakhtin wrote:

> Carnival is not a spectacle seen by the people; they live in it, and everyone participates because its very idea embraces all the people . . . During carnival time life is subject only to its laws, that is, the laws of its own freedom.[20]

For women, such freedom meant the opportunity to take the initiative – in speech as well as actions. In *The Rover* this could be due, in part, to Behn's use of Killigrew's text (which is freer than most in this respect) and, particularly, her reassignment to Hellena of certain speeches which Killigrew allocated to a male character. When the play opens, she has already resolved to find a man and initiate a relationship: her father and brother may be planning to save the cost of a dowry by placing her in a convent, but she is quite aware of what she has to offer – and to gain by making other plans. Her sister, Florinda, has already determined to defy their father and refuses to marry 'the rich old Don Vincentio', being equally sure of her worth (I.i.16–22).

Both are set for battle when their brother enters – apparently not noticing Hellena at first and addressing only Florinda – which suggests that he believes the novice to be elsewhere praying, an impression reinforced by his surprise when she cannot resist butting into the conversation to take Florinda's part. Hellena not only disobeys his command to 'Go – up to your devotion' (he leaves before she does), but she fiercely challenges everything he says, mocks Vincentio's lack of virility, and shocks Pedro with her tenacity ('Have you done yet?'), and her outspoken language. Behn toned down Killigrew's description of the old prospective husband who 'farts as loud as a Musket for a jest' to 'sighs a belch or two,

20 Mikhail Bakhtin, *Rabelais and his World*; trans. Helene Iswolsky, Bloomington, Indiana, 1984, p. 7.

loud as a musket', but reserved the detail for greater impact later in Hellena's outraged, 'What then? The viceroy's son is better than that old Sir Fisty'. Pedro, shocked by his sister's disrespectful term (old fart)[21] for her father's choice of husband, orders her immediate incarceration for the duration of the carnival followed, at Lent, by 'her everlasting penance in a monastery'. For Hellena, the carnival has already begun: she is indulging in vigorous colloquial outspokenness – her free expression of oaths ('Now hang me if . . . ' I.i.23), and her skills of witty mockery make her a natural sparring partner for the outspoken Willmore. Hellena looks to the carnival to provide her with experience of love and life and, as Elin Diamond aptly expresses it, 'She exercises her will only by pursuing and winning Willmore, for as it turns out he has the "more" she "would fain know"'.[22]

Willmore steps ashore in search of 'Love and mirth' in a 'warm climate' after having been deprived of women and good living onboard ship. He may stink 'of tar and ropes' ends like a dock or pesthouse' (I.ii.92–3) but he has an abundance of persuasive rhetoric as well as desire: 'I have a world of love in store. Would you would . . . take some on't off my hands' (I.ii.147–9). While he has been confined to male company at sea, Hellena has been pent up in a nunnery and, like him, she is eager to start making up for lost time (I.ii.182–3). She has no intention of dying 'a maid, and in a captain's hands too' (V.i.413), but the liberality of carnival does not mean that she has forgotten the realities of everyday life. Hellena's gipsy disguise *is* only a disguise: she does not really want a life of hardship and 'A cradle full of noise and mischief, with a pack of repentance at my back' (V.i.444–5). Her plain speaking and scorn of Willmore's attempts to win her, persuade him into a marriage 'bargain' which, although both enter defensively, she has engineered. Perhaps marriage is as unattractive to her as it is to Willmore but, without it, the freedom to explore her sexual desires could take her back to the convent as an abandoned, unmarriageable young woman, with or without a child.

Another freedom of carnival is the opportunity to act foolishly without regard to social position. In, finally, not opposing his sisters' marriages, Don Pedro bows to the prevailing pressures of festivity. Wickedly, Behn allows him to relish his liberation from patriarchal responsibility. When we first meet Pedro he is about to put on his masked costume and

21 See textual note to I.i.133. This is not the only reading, but it is plausible – and less tautological than the alternative.

22 Elin Diamond, 'Gestus and signature in Aphra Behn's *The Rover*', *ELH* (56), 1989, 528. See also David M. Sullivan, 'The female will in Aphra Behn', *Women's Studies* 22 (1993), 335–47.

participate in revels he has forbidden to his sisters. By the end, in forgiving everyone, he has entered into the spirit of equality which characterises carnival life. One by one, male and female alike, the characters venture out: Florinda and Belvile to find each other, Hellena and Valeria to woo husbands, Pedro and Antonio to win Angellica, Blunt to seek an inexpensive woman, and Willmore to take any woman. Those who achieve their desires do so by complicated routes, often involving potential humiliation and risk: others are exposed to ridicule, danger and defeat. Antonio is wounded and Belvile, a victim of mistaken identity, is driven to participate in the equivalent of a carnivalesque mock duel. All are free to play the fool for a time, but if any person could be considered to have been elected King of Fools by his companions, that person must be Blunt.

He is victimised by Lucetta, Philippo, and Sancho in additional ways to those found in Killigrew's text, where his counterpart, Edwardo, is merely turned out of doors in his drawers in the night and is lost in the city streets by the equivalent of Sancho. Bakhtin notes that carnival hell included, amongst other things, a trap to catch fools, and Behn adds a Rabelaisian touch to Blunt's debasement by dropping him literally into excrement. On one level the foolish country fop becomes a hero of folk humour when he falls down the trapdoor into the sewer and undergoes a mock journey to the underworld, returning to tell of the horrors he found there. At another level, Blunt's fate can be seen as a veiled political comment. It is wished on him in I.ii by Frederick when, having noticed Blunt's disappearance in pursuit of Lucetta, he declares,

> I hope 'tis some common crafty sinner, one that will fit him. It may be she'll sell him for Peru: the rogue's sturdy, and would work well in a mine. At least I hope she'll dress him for our mirth, cheat him of all, then have him well-favouredly banged, and turned out naked at midnight. (I.ii.270–4)

The reason for Frederick's uncharacteristic vindictiveness becomes clear when Belvile catalogues details of Blunt's privileged upbringing. Never having known hardship or the sordid side of life, never having committed himself to a cause as they have done, and, therefore, never having risked life, limb, or fortune, the wealthy 'Essex calf' is a cause of deep-seated resentment – though this is usually over-ridden by good humour. It is as if the spirit of carnival allows Frederick's idle wish to be granted. Blunt is not sold to labour in a Peruvian mine, but he is forced underground and exposed to other nightmare experiences. He is also subjected to the carnivalesque removal of his fine clothes and their replacement with a clown-like costume – his underwear and 'an old rusty sword and buff belt'. His horrified response, 'Now, how like a morris dancer I am equipped!' (IV.v.7–8), and his equally disgusted view of himself in the Spanish habit he is forced to wear later, signifies his humiliation. Belvile's pronouncement on the new costume is telling: 'Methinks 'tis well, and makes thee look e'en cavalier' (V.i.543). Finally, even the Englishmen are equal – Blunt, with his possible parliamentarian leanings and fastidious fussing about his clothes, has at last to make-do like one of the cavaliers.

In carnival time costume is crucial, and from the first scene of *The Rover* characters are changing their clothes and exchanging identities for a variety of purposes. When a character loses control of their state of dress, as in the case of Blunt and, later, of Florinda, who escapes to the garden 'in an undress' (III.v), their vulnerability is apparent. Hellena, however, always appears to have the situation in hand and makes successful transitions from novice's garb to gipsy costume, and finally to the boy's clothes she is wearing when Willmore agrees to marry her. Female cross-dressing was popular on the Restoration stage as a means of allowing the audience to view more of the woman playing the part, so Behn may have merely been catering to audience expectations here, but Willmore's possible associations with the Earl of Rochester and John Hoyle, both of whom pursued men as well as women, probably gave her choice an additional *frisson*. Historically, there is also a link between women who adopted male attire and certain prostitutes who used such dress to signal their profession. There is no indication that Hellena's appearance would have been viewed in this way, but the ambiguous natures of costume and masquerade in the play also reveal the dangers of judging by appearances.

Outsiders

Most of *The Rover*'s characters are outsiders of one kind or another: Naples is under Spanish rule, Angellica Bianca is introduced as a native of Padua, even the English are divided into the impecunious cosmopolitan cavaliers and the wealthy traveller from the country, whom they befriend but constantly taunt because he never committed himself politically and kept his privileges and estate. Willmore is not just a rover – a pirate, one who wanders, an inconstant lover – he is a 'Tramontana rover' (V.i.378) which, apart from signifying someone uncouth, indicates a foreigner or stranger. Established incomers prey upon more recent arrivals: Lucetta exploits Blunt's ignorance of Naples and of her ways – though she does worry that her treatment of him may put paid to future dealings with foreigners if word gets around (III.iii.46–7). The protagonists are all away from their home ground and are vulnerable because of this. The usual social hierarchies are inverted. The Spanish, old enemies of the English, are either in power officially (Don Antonio is the viceroy's son) or unofficially (Philippo takes the spoils Lucetta tricks from Blunt and reminds us of the old quarrel about the Spanish Armada in his reference to 'old Queen Bess's' gold and the 'quarrel . . . since eighty-eight' (III.iii.41–2). The English, who might have been gentlemen at home, are poor, riotous, and often despised abroad.

Although the victimisation of prostitutes was a common feature of traditional carnival, Behn does not condemn either Lucetta or Angellica Bianca but rather, at significant moments, gives them the upper hand over the English strangers, an even more disadvantaged and male social group. No matter how brave they may be, abroad they are distinguished principally by their lack of riches and often run-down appearance; even a courtesan's servant feels free to mock Willmore in his presence (II.ii.19–20). Blunt has managed to retain his wealth, being no cavalier, yet he does not have the wit to keep it and escape abuse. Lucetta soon picks him out as a gullible fool:

> He's English too, and they say that's a sort of good-natured loving people, and have generally so kind an opinion of themselves that a woman with any wit may flatter 'em into any sort of fool she pleases. (I.ii.197–200)

This is gender specific, unlike the jibe in *Hamlet* that the English are all mad: Behn's joke implies that, at home and abroad, an English male is no match for any woman's wit.

Daring Women, Courtesans and Prostitutes

The shift that took place in Restoration comedy, from a focus on the male lead to an awareness that 'his lady' was the real 'centre of interest',[23] is apparent in George Etherege's *The Man of Mode*, which was performed the year before *The Rover*. This transition coincided with Behn's influence on contemporary theatre as a female playwright and the advent of women (rather than the boy actors of earlier times) playing female roles after 1660. *The Rover* begins by focusing on women: it opens with Hellena and Florinda discussing their lack of independence while confidently expressing their opinions and desires. Only Lucetta, of all the females in

23 Donald Bruce, *Topics of Restoration Comedy*, New York, 1974, p. 135.

the play, seems unable to do this – perhaps because she merely exploits the carnival spirit for financial gain at the command of Philippo and is always under his control. Like Angellica, Lucetta demonstrates how difficult it is for women – especially kept-women and prostitutes – to retain their sexual freedom. Dependent on men financially for their survival, they cannot afford the luxury of dispensing favours at will. Angellica, with her greater independence and wealth, fares better than Lucetta. She also, like Hellena and Florinda, has the advantage of a female ally. Her woman, Moretta, is probably motivated more by economic considerations than emotional attachment, but we feel sure that when Angellica finally turns her back on Willmore, Moretta will be there to help her return to her old, confident state. Similarly, in I.i Hellena fiercely takes her sister's part in criticising their father's wishes and her brother's intentions to carry them out; later, Valeria rushes to the rescue when Hellena and Florinda find themselves under threat. Supportive, energetic women are Behn's speciality.

Behn was not only unusual in giving prostitution so much attention in her plays, but she also frequently tackled the topic of arranged marriage in which women and money were exchanged in a different kind of bargain. From her first play, *The Forced Marriage*, she championed a woman's right to choose her own husband. The issue was to reappear at least eleven times in her dramatic works. *The Rover* highlights the double standards normally practised by both men and women. A society in which rich old men take young wives they cannot satisfy, encourages the latter to 'ramble to supply the defects of some grave, impotent husband' (IV.v.72–3) and allows women like Lucetta to use this as a cover for deception and robbery. When, as Belvile insists, there are wealthy 'whores' who do not fit the traditional stereotype, and wealthy wives doing much the same but without the fee, how is a man like Blunt to discern whether he is predator or prey?

> Why yes, sir, they are whores, though they'll neither entertain you with drinking, swearing, or bawdry; are whores in all those gay clothes and right jewels . . . with those great houses richly furnished . . . are whores, and arrant ones. (II.i.71–5)

In the carnival, as Willmore and Belvile show Blunt, there are also 'Fine pretty creatures' who 'would have you think they're courtesans . . . ' (I.ii.79–82). By drawing attention in the drama to a confusion that extended from carnival into life beyond the play, Behn makes her audience question notions of respectability and notoriety in relation to women's sexuality. Nancy Copeland sees Behn's juxtapositioning of Hellena and Angellica resulting 'in a narrowing of the distance between virgin and whore that complicates the final rejection of the courtesan and her ultimate exclusion from the play's comic conclusion'.[24] In many ways these characters are two sides of the same coin: both advertise their attractions to Willmore and pursue him in different fashions; both are willing to subsidise his poverty with money from the same source (Hellena's fortune comes from her uncle who was Angellica's 'Spanish general'); and both offer themselves to him for love. They differ mainly in the way they view that concept in relationships between men and women. Ironically, the worldly courtesan is less astute than the convent girl in assessing the nature of a rover like Willmore. In depriving Angellica of her man, Behn is not taking a moral stand: Angellica, the romantic, must give way to Hellena, the realist, who will provide her revenge. Angellica's future is left undetermined but Behn gives her the opportunity to express herself eloquently and provoke sympathy. Love, like carnival madness, has its darker side – and in carnival everyone has a voice. When Behn wrote *The Rover* part II, a widowed Willmore this time chose the courtesan rather than the gentlewoman. Elizabeth Barry, who had played Hellena, also played his later love, La Nuche, so a connection between courtesan and noblewoman continued.

Since men like Blunt and Willmore regard any unprotected woman as being sexually available, regardless of what they are told, Hellena is particularly daring when she first hears about Florinda's love for Belvile and declares, 'I hope he has some mad companion or other that will spoil my devotion' (I.i.33–5). From that point on she exerts all her energies to provoke an assault on her virginity, advertising it at every opportunity, confident that she has the wit to handle the situation to her ultimate advantage. Florinda, on the other hand, is constantly fending off attempted rape from the time of her first meeting with Belvile, 'when I was exposed to such dangers as the licensed lust of common soldiers threatened when rage and conquest flew through the city' (I.i.70–2). The Englishmen like to think they are no common soldiers intent on rape and pillage, but in Willmore's drunken assault on Florinda in III.v and the mass rape planned in Act IV by Blunt with the compliance, at one point, of Frederick and the others, a modern audience may begin to doubt. While indecent behaviour towards women is part of the carnival tradition and Restoration drama frequently incorporates a physical assault on a virtuous heroine (even Nahum Tate's rewriting of *King Lear*

24 Nancy Copeland, '"Once a whore and ever"? Whore and virgin in *The Rover* and its antecedents', *Restoration: Studies in English Literary Culture, 1660–1700*, 16 (1992), 21.

includes an attempted rape of Cordelia), Behn's treatment of the issue raises far-reaching questions concerning sexual violence against women[25] (particularly of different social stations) and the problems involved in the way female chastity was prized, protected, and put under siege.

The men perpetuate a situation where the honour of their own women is valued and fiercely defended, but a female without an effective protector is seen as fair game or, as Willmore puts it, 'another prize' (III.i.281). When circumstances temporarily remove a woman from family or marital protection, the men become victims of each others' prejudices and lusts. For all his boasting, Frederick is inexperienced; he acts according to the primitive distinctions that governed much male behaviour at the time, 'I begin to suspect something; and 'twould anger us vilely to be trussed up for a rape upon a maid of quality, when we only believe we ruffle a harlot' (IV.v.124–6). The 'harlot' is, of course, Florinda: Frederick's description of her earlier as 'that damned virtuous woman' (I.ii.18–19) is almost realised. The farce which provokes both laughter and unease as the masked Florinda is physically threatened by one male after another, reaches its climax when her own brother, who has been the fiercest defender of her honour, draws the longest sword in the contest to take possession of her body. Belvile is helpless and only the timely intervention of Valeria saves the day. The ridiculous situation was brought about by Don Pedro's insistence that Florinda should marry the man of his choosing rather than her own and that Hellena should be denied marriage altogether. Finally, Florinda's match is a *fait accompli* and the strain of making a stand against that of Willmore and Hellena is too great. Don Pedro consents in the face of mass resistance, relieved to 'be free from fears of her honour'; 'guard it you now, if you can', he tells Willmore, 'I have been a slave to't long enough' (V.i.518–19). Willmore's advice that 'a woman's honour is not worth guarding when she has a mind to part with it' (V.i.520–22) could be said to be the message of the play.

Both Lucetta and Angellica are victims of a male-centred society and an economy which treats women as a commodity, but each has her own methods of survival built on compromise and they manipulate the men on whom they depend. The 'jilting wench', Lucetta, gains great wealth without giving any favours to a country gentleman, while the 'famous courtesan' who demands a ridiculously high price, eventually chooses to bestow herself for nothing on a penniless pirate and, when she cannot command his constant love, holds him at pistol point to revenge her honour.

25 See Ann Marie Stewart, *The Ravishing Restoration: Aphra Behn, Violence, and Comedy*, Selinsgrove, PA, 2010, for an appendix that lists Behn's plays which include rape or attempted rape.

Angellica may not win Willmore, yet she retains his admiration and the adoration and respect of someone as rich and powerful as the viceroy's son. Behn's women reserve the right to adjust their monetary price as it suits them, being more financially secure than many of the men in the play. Even the upright Belvile is dependent on marrying into money.

The box of jewels which Florinda hides in the garden may be a metaphor for the virtue she has so much difficulty preserving, but since Jessica's flight to Lorenzo in Shakespeare's *The Merchant of Venice*, it is also a symbol of the defiant woman who breaks through family and cultural opposition to give herself and her wealth to the man of her choice. Angellica is not the only woman to use her own portrait to draw a man to her. At III.i.258, Florinda gives her picture (inside a jewel) to Belvile as encouragement. Whether courtesan or noblewoman, taking the initiative means taking risks. Florinda dares to unlock the gate of the walled garden to meet her lover, but the danger of such an action is demonstrated when Willmore, rather than Belvile enters. However, it is the women who, finally, arrange the men's futures. Even the woman-shy Frederick has his fate determined by Florinda, who agrees to be reconciled with him if he will fulfil Valeria's desires and marry, 'a maid that does not hate you, and whose fortune (I believe) will not be unwelcome to you' (V.i.159–61).

The Play on the Stage

In Behn's Lifetime

Behn's first plays, *The Forced Marriage* (1670) and *The Amorous Prince* (1671), were performed by the Duke's Company at Lincoln's Inn Fields, but *The Dutch Lover* (1673), the tragedy *Abdelazer*, and the comedy *The Town Fop* (both 1676), *The Debauchee* and *The Counterfeit Bridegroom* (both attributed to Behn and dated 1677), and *The Rover* (1677) were produced at Christopher Wren's Duke's Theatre,[26] Dorset Garden, as were all her later plays until *The Lucky Chance* (1686) and *The Emperor of the Moon* (1687) came out at Drury Lane. *The Widow Ranter* and *The Younger Brother* were both produced there posthumously, in 1689 and 1696 respectively.

Restoration theatres seated up to approximately 800 people.[27] The Duke's Theatre, Dorset Garden, had a proscenium stage and an acting

26 Simon Trussler in *An Adaptation of The Rover by Aphra Behn*, London, 1986, p. 11. Edward A. Langhans suggests Robert Hooke as designer of The Duke's Theatre in *LTW*, p. 62.

27 See J.L. Styan, *Restoration Comedy in Performance*, Cambridge, 1986, pp. 20–21.

space which extended forward from the curtain line, with doors and balcony spaces on both sides. Most of the action probably took place on the forestage, nearest the audience. Reconstructions of the theatre by Edward A. Langhans suggest that this area was 19′6″ (5.9 metres) deep, with a proscenium width of 30′6″ (9.3 metres) and a total stage depth of 51′ (15.5 metres).[28] Apart from the introduction of women to act female parts, the main advance in the Restoration period was painted background scenery, moved along grooves or tracks by machines. A number of these shutters would be used, so that one pair could be drawn back to reveal another in place behind them and so change the setting, for example from one street to another, as at IV.iv. Behind the shutters was a discovery space, where characters could be 'discovered' or revealed: for example, the opening stage direction of IV.i reads, '*A fine room. Discovers* BELVILE *as by dark alone*'. The shutters and the area behind them constitute the 'scene' and at IV.iii.62 we find the stage direction '*Enter* FLORINDA *from the farther end of the scene, looking behind her*'. The space behind the shutters could be extended right to the back wall of the theatre to create 'long' scenes, using wings to form a perspective converging on the farthest wall. Either this or a perspective painting of a street would have been used for the 'long street' specified at I.ii and II.i.

It was common to have a large, mechanically-operated trapdoor upstage, to raise or lower properties such as the bed in III.iii, but Dorset Garden was relatively unusual in being able to darken its stage, perhaps by lowering the footlights below stage level. This effect may have been reserved for spectacles such as occurred in Dryden and Davenant's version of *The Tempest*,[29] and may not have been in general use, but the impact of Florinda's encounter with the drunken Willmore, for example, would have differed depending on whether the audience could see actions and expressions clearly (which seems most likely), or whether the impression was one of voices and an indistinct scuffle. The usual practice in theatres at this time was to keep both stage and house lights fully operational throughout a performance and to suggest darkness on-stage through the use of candles or torches, as employed later in III.v (e.g. '*Enter* PEDRO . . . *with lights*', l. 80). Willmore's, 'by this light' (l.15) is an asseverative phrase, i.e. 'by this [good] light', which refers to the moon: he is not carrying a lantern.

The first recorded performance of *The Rover* at the Duke's Theatre was on 24 March 1677 and Charles II was present. Jacqueline Pearson

28 *LWT*, p. 62.
29 This was Shadwell's operatic production at Dorset Garden in 1674. See Colin Visser, 'Scenery and technical design' in *LTW*, p. 113.

comments on Behn's technique in casting a 'known married couple', Thomas and Mary Betterton, as Belvile and Florinda, 'to maintain comic equilibrium in a play where Florinda is constantly in danger of rape'. In contrast, Elizabeth Barry, twenty years younger and at the start of her career, was cast as Hellena and William Smith, later known for his Jacobite sympathies, as 'the royalist Willmore'.[30] The play was a success, being revived at court in 1680, 1685, 1687, and 1690, and at either Drury Lane or Dorset Garden in 1685.

Later Productions and Adaptations

The Rover remained popular after Behn's death: 165 performances are recorded between 1700 and 1790.[31] After this it reappeared as *Love in Many Masks*, a toned-down version by John Philip Kemble in 1790, which indicates that theatrical tastes had changed. Behn's play appears to have been out of favour in the nineteenth century, and was neglected for the majority of the twentieth century, despite Montague Summers's edition in 1915. The Feminist Movement, which focused attention on the works of hitherto forgotten women writers, eventually brought *The Rover* back to prominence and there were several productions of the play in the late 1970s and early 1980s in America and the UK, but its first major twentieth-century production was due to the opening of The Swan Theatre, Stratford-upon-Avon, a new Royal Shakespeare Theatre Company venue dedicated to staging a more comprehensive range of sixteenth- and seventeenth-century plays than had been possible previously.

The director, John Barton, like Kemble, thought there was a need to rework Behn's text, and he produced his own edition by cutting 550 lines, adding 350 (some of these came from *Thomaso*, but others he supplied himself), and rearranging the structure and setting.[32] The Swan Theatre, where Barton's production was first performed in July 1986, despite the lack of a proscenium arch and painted 'scenes', may have reproduced some staging conditions similar to Dorset Garden, putting actors and audience in intimate proximity, providing a side balcony for Angellica, a trap door for Blunt, and a stage full of energetic women (Imogen Stubbs played Hellena; Geraldine Fitzgerald, Florinda; and Sinead Cusack, Angellica). However, by transforming Belvile into 'a black soldier of

30 Pearson, op. cit. p. 52.

31 William van Lennep, ed., *Index to The London Stage, 1660–1880*, Carbondale and Edwardsville, 1979, p. 61.

32 John Barton, *An Adaptation of The Rover by Aphra Behn*; programme /text with commentary by Simon Trussler, Methuen, 1986. See also Nancy Copeland, 'Re-Producing *The Rover*: John Barton's *Rover* at the Swan', *Essays in Theatre* 9 (1990), 45–60.

fortune', setting the play in an unnamed Spanish colony, expanding several characters' roles (most notably that of Valeria, who became the sister of Hellena and Florinda), and altering both the beginning and the ending, this version differed from Behn's in important ways.

By reverting to Killigrew's opening scene, Barton focused initially on male interests rather than female. Jeremy Irons's swashbuckling Willmore looked the part as the pirate but for some his 'flourishing first entrance' exaggerated 'the potential, which certainly exists in Behn's play, for glorification of the rover'.[33] Although Hellena claims she finds Willmore's 'unconstant humour' attractive (IV.ii,199), a modern audience may be less willing to indulge his urges to pounce on any young female he encounters, and more inclined to agree with the exasperated Belvile when he demands, 'Must you be a beast – a brute, a senseless swine?' (III.vi.2–3). This production played the assaults on Florinda primarily for comic effect, choosing not to assert that Behn's rover is a drunken would-be rapist (III.v) and a hot-headed blunderer (IV.ii.89), as well as a tarnished hero. Similarly, Barton rearranged the ending so that it was almost a case of *Oronooko* meets *The Three [Restoration] Musketeers*. Before Belvile's final couplets to King Charles and the future marriages came the stage direction: '*All shed their Carnival gear, the Masquers all appearing as slaves and such like, and go out singing a working song*'. As a festive comedy, this version had many strengths and was highly enjoyable to watch, but it was not Behn's play. Nevertheless, the production was a success and transferred to the Mermaid Theatre, London.

Barton's text has continued to be performed amongst a variety of productions of *The Rover* on stages all over the world. These include those by the State Theatre Company of South Australia (1989 and 1990), the Mercury Theatre Auckland, New Zealand (1989), and the New Cross Theatre, Goldsmiths College (1991). The latter was particularly successful in demonstrating Behn's ambivalent portrayal of Willmore, and stressed the lack of safety, for both men and women, in an environment where danger and violence are commonplace. Elizabeth Schafer notes that, 'In Gale Edward's production of *The Rover* (State Theatre Company of South Australia, 1989 and 1990) Willmore was sometimes booed and hissed'[34] – and in a production by the Women's Playhouse Trust at London's Jacob Street Film Studios in October 1994 the tension created in IV.v, as both Blunt and Frederick prepared to rape Florinda, proved that though the audience knew them to be foolish and inexperienced comic characters, it could not banish the deep unease which their actions provoked. Even

33 Elizabeth Schafer, 'Appropriating Aphra', *Australasian Drama Studies* 19 (1991), 43.
34 Ibid., 49.

so, this production was not as feminist as might have been expected; the male characters were treated sympathetically even when most undeserving, with the emphasis on male weaknesses rather than vindictiveness. This is true to the way Behn demonstrates both an awareness of male injustice to women and an acknowledgement of female attraction to fickle men. However, she provokes most laughter at the expense of her male, not female, characters.

The Rover frequently places vulnerable men and women in enclosed interiors (Florinda and Hellena in I.i, Angellica in II.ii, Belvile in IV.i, Blunt in IV.v, and Florinda in IV.v and V.i), and the vast circus ring of London's Jacob Street Film Studios was less effective in this respect than a traditional theatre space, until the scenes concerning Blunt and Florinda. In these, huge nets were let down from the roof to form four walls, and first Blunt, then Florinda found themselves trapped like helpless animals in a cage or insects in a web. Florinda's unfortunate attempt to take refuge in Blunt's chamber became a visual reminder that the 'cobweb door set open . . . to catch flies' (which, earlier, Willmore had ironically associated with Florinda in a predatory role, III.v.55) can snare naive virgins as well as sexually-tempted men like Blunt.

The WPT production (in association with the Open University and the BBC) was geared both to exploring the text in ways which were relevant to a multi-cultural society, and to making it available on stage and on video. The most striking aspect of the performance was the ease with which the play appeared able to accommodate and represent a number of different cultures simultaneously. On one hand, Behn is specific in her references to the English, Spanish, and Italians, and the play is a lively exposé of the English in Europe in the 1650s. On the other hand, her understanding of life in a society comprising such disparate groups of individuals, and her perception concerning male–female relations, allow *The Rover* to transcend historical and geographical restrictions.[35] The Women's Playhouse Trust set their production in India: it encompassed a wide range of black cultures as well as an 'English' band with a variety of accents, including Irish.

There were weaknesses: a thick carpet of sand suggested heat and a holiday sense of the exotic, but the clouds of dust which rose whenever a rickshaw bowled past or a fight took place were a challenge for both actors and audience. Nevertheless, the pioneering spirit of *The Rover* remained triumphant. One of the leading Kathakali dancers in India,

35 Gyllian Raby's adaptation for Memorial University, Newfoundland (1996) set *The Rover* in 1938 during the Spanish Civil War; the Queen's Company set it in the American Civil War (New York, 2001).

Maya Krishna Rao, played Angellica as a sensuous temptress in a pavilion created beneath a floating purple veil. Her seduction techniques could hardly have differed more from those of Cecilia Noble's Hellena, as she raced around the arena on a bicycle in pursuit of Willmore. In staging *The Rover* the WPT demonstrated that it is possible to bring an exciting celebration of carnival and a meaningful exploration of gender and social issues together.

Over ten years later, *The Rover*'s appeal appeared to be undiminished with numerous performances worldwide in 2005.[36] One of the most innovative of these was an adaptation by Josh Costello, who also directed it for the Chance Theater in Anaheim, California.[37] In this, Behn's play (with some cuts, a few lines from *Thomaso*, and even a couple from Shakespeare's plays in the introduction) was enacted by four 15 year old girls on a sleepover or slumber party, who used their imaginations and what they had to hand – a dressing-up chest and some dolls and puppets. Their skilled manipulation of the latter unexpectedly brought Don Pedro to life as a dog with long drooping ears and a serious expression, while Barbie and Ken dolls were effectively used to dramatise Blunt's encounter with Lucetta. Alex Bueno, Emily Clark, Vanessa Martinez and Barbara Suiter leapt in and out of their shared bunk beds (poised on top of low bookshelves), donning masks, wigs, and makeshift costumes to transport their audience back to Behn's time, occasionally breaking the spell to demonstrate the way the girls were taken over by their imaginations. Despite the lively humour that pervaded this production and the all-female cast, the potential threat of rape in III.v was menacingly conveyed. In its novel exploration of gender roles and the female imagination, Costello's thought-provoking adaptation marked another successful transformation of *The Rover* on the contemporary stage. It was performed again in 2006 by the Dallas Hub Theatre, Texas, directed by Christie Shane, and may eventually prove to be the successor to Barton's adaptation.[38]

36 2005 productions include those of the Centurion Theatre Company (London), Magdalen College (Oxford), the Royal Welsh College of Music and Drama, the University of Alberta Studio Theatre, Kalamazoo College, Michigan, the Humber School of Creative and Performing Arts, California, and Josh Costello's adaptation for the Chance Theater, Orange County, California.

37 The Chance Theater also produced a television broadcast for KOCE-TV. See www.joshcostello.com for more details of his adaptation.

38 For further discussion of this adaptation see Nancy Copeland, 'Aphra Behn in the Contemporary Theater' in *Teaching British Women Playwrights of the Restoration and Eighteenth Century*, eds. Bonnie Nelson & Catherine Burroughs, New York, 2010, pp. 77–9.

There have been over a dozen productions of *The Rover* in the UK and America in the last five years. These have played on the links between Rochester and Elizabeth Barry (Hunter Productions at London's Tabard Theatre and the Edinburgh Fringe in 2007), relocated the action to Venice and (with varying success) divided the performance between a theatre bar, with swordfights erupting amongst drinkers, and the traditional theatre space (the Southwark Playhouse, London, in 2009), and taken the audience on a panoramic promenade on multiple stages in a three and a half acre complex at the World Arts Financial Center (New York Classical Theatre, 2011). *The Rover*'s appeal to contemporary directors and audiences shows no sign of diminishing – it is particularly popular today with all-female and youth companies.

A Summary of the Plot

Set in Naples at carnival time, *The Rover* opens with sisters, Florinda and Hellena, talking of love. Hellena's father and brother (Don Pedro) expect her to be a nun, although this does not suit her. They also plan to marry Florinda to a rich old suitor, Don Vincentio (her father's choice), or the wealthy Don Antonio, the viceroy's son (her brother's choice), but she is in love with an impoverished, banished English colonel, Don Belvile. Don Pedro intends to confine Hellena for the duration of the carnival and to make Florinda marry the following day. In retaliation, the sisters and their governess, Callis, join the revels.

English cavaliers in exile (Belvile, Blunt and Frederick) are joined by Willmore, a dashing rover who has just come ashore for the carnival. Florinda, Hellena and their kinswoman, Valeria, arrive with Callis, disguised as gipsies. They share the stage with Lucetta, her gallant, Philippo, and Sancho, Lucetta's pimp. Lucetta targets Blunt for his money. Florinda asks Belvile to meet her at the garden gate that night. Willmore arranges to meet Hellena. Blunt goes off with Lucetta. The other Englishmen talk of Angellica Bianca, former mistress of a dead Spanish general, who has advertised herself for sale at a monthly rate.

In Act II, Belvile and Frederick are in masking disguise and Willmore carries a vizard. Blunt has been intoxicated by the deceitful Lucetta. While they admire Angellica's picture which she has displayed, Don Pedro enters in his masking costume. Angellica plays the lute and sings, then throws open her curtains and bows to Don Antonio. Willmore steals her picture and fights with the Spaniards. The other Englishmen join in. Willmore is wounded and enters Angellica's house, despite the other men's warnings. He desires Angellica but cannot afford her. She says that she would not consider him even if he were wealthy. Nevertheless, they are mutually attracted – in spirit as well as physically. He seduces her and she agrees that he can pay with love. She also gives him five hundred crowns.

In Act III, Florinda, Valeria and Hellena are disguised when Belvile, Blunt and Frederick appear. Willmore enters, apparently enthralled by Angellica, and this vexes Hellena. Sancho leads Blunt off to see Lucetta while Hellena returns as a gipsy and takes on Willmore. As he seems to court Hellena, Angellica enters with other maskers. Hellena removes her mask briefly and captivates Willmore but this makes Angellica jealous. She tells Sebastian to follow Hellena and discover her identity. Lucetta and Sancho trick and rob Blunt, dropping him through a trap door wearing only his underclothes. He escapes through the sewer. Willmore, now drunk, stumbles upon Florinda (waiting to meet Belvile) and forces himself on her. She resists but he treats her like a prostitute and tries to pay her with a paltry amount. She is rescued from Willmore's attempted rape by Belvile. Her brother is alerted and a fight ensues. Belvile challenges Willmore to a duel, which is delayed. Meanwhile, Antonio pays Angellica for her favours but Willmore draws his sword and they fight. Antonio is injured and Belvile, mistakenly blamed, is seized by soldiers.

In Act IV, Antonio offers to pardon Belvile if he will fight a rival for him. Belvile enters, disguised as Antonio, to fight Don Pedro, who believes Don Antonio has slighted Florinda by preferring Angellica. Belvile offers to fight but Florinda runs in and is discovered by her brother. Don Pedro is satisfied that the man he believes to be Antonio has proved he loves Florinda – so he gives her to him and proposes that they marry quickly. Willmore rushes in, recognises Belvile, and knocks off his vizard so that Don Pedro realises his mistake and takes Florinda back. Belvile is furious with Willmore, who draws his sword against Pedro. Belvile separates them but Pedro leaves with Florinda. Belvile turns on Willmore as Angellica enters, also furious with Willmore. She accuses him of courting Hellena for her wealth. On learning that his 'gipsy' is rich, Willmore is impressed. Hellena enters, disguised as a boy, and goes to Angellica, who makes Willmore stay to listen. In disguise, Hellena claims that she is related to one who loves Willmore. He denies this but Angellica is not convinced. He tries to find out the name of his admirer from Hellena, secretly, and fails her test of his fidelity. When he learns it is his 'gipsy' that she means, he belittles her to Angellica – but is still eager to rush off to meet her later. Angellica leaves, resolving to be revenged.

Florinda and Valeria enter, newly disguised, looking for Hellena. Don Pedro, Belvile and Willmore encounter them and Willmore takes an interest in Valeria. Frederick brings news of Blunt's duping. Florinda is trying to evade her brother. Valeria follows Willmore out (in disguise) and Hellena shadows them both. To hide from her brother, Florinda accidentally goes into the lodgings Belvile shares with the other Englishmen and Willmore loses sight of Valeria. Blunt has made it back to his chamber where he sits in his underclothes, plotting revenge. He is reading, armed with an old rusty sword, when Florinda wanders in. Still smarting from his experience with Lucetta, Blunt treats her roughly, threatening to beat, rape and rob her in revenge. Frederick enters and Blunt invites him to take part. In desperation, Florinda mentions Belvile's name and shows them her diamond ring. They agree to wait for Belvile and Frederick takes Florinda away.

In Act V, Belvile, Willmore and Pedro seek out Blunt, who tells them about the woman he found. Blunt shows Belvile the ring and he realises that their captive is Florinda, but dares not reveal this. The men draw swords for her, forgetting that Don Pedro's Toledo will be the longest. A masked Florinda enters running – pursued by her brother. Valeria distracts Pedro by saying that Florinda has fled, disguised as a page, and urges him to find her. She then encourages Florinda and Belvile to marry quickly. Willmore and the rest learn all and make peace with Florinda. Frederick is matched with Valeria. The couples leave to find a priest.

In masking dress, Angellica threatens to kill Willmore with a pistol – then she pulls off her vizard. She accuses him of breaking his vows. He expresses admiration for her and offers to return her gold. She still means to shoot him but Antonio disarms her. When he recognises Willmore as the thief who stole her painting, he himself offers to shoot him. Angellica intervenes, lets Willmore live, and leaves. Antonio is detained by Pedro and the confusion of the duel is explained. Pedro threatens to give Florinda to Belvile in revenge but learns that they are already married without his consent. When Belvile returns, Pedro relents and wishes them well. They leave to find Florinda as Hellena arrives. Willmore recognises her as his gipsy. Pedro arrives to object but Hellena declares she wants to marry Willmore so Pedro, over-ruled by the assembled crowd, gives her to him. Blunt offers his allegiance to Hellena. The play ends with music and a masked dance, all threats of violence dispelled.

Note on the Text

The first Quarto was the only edition of *The Rover* to be printed during Aphra Behn's lifetime and forms the basis for subsequent quarto editions in 1697 (Q2) and 1709 (Q3), an octavo printed in 1737, a duodecimo in 1741, and a reworking by Kemble in 1790. A two-volume collected edition of Aphra Behn's plays, based on Q2, appeared in 1702 (C) and was reissued in a single volume in 1716. A further edition in four volumes (C2) came out in 1724 and was the basis of two more editions in 1871 and 1915. Until Frederick M. Link's useful edition in 1967, which went back to the authoritative first Quarto, *The Rover* had been reproduced for centuries in a variety of corrupt texts. The present edition is based on the first Quarto, and any substantive variations from it are recorded in the textual notes. Not all variants from Q2, Q3, C and C2 are listed, but any which offer plausible alternative readings are included. The original spelling of characters' names is retained, though in some cases this has had to be regularised; other spellings have been modernised, as has punctuation, but substantive variations from Q1 are noted. Q1 employs a large number of dashes, sometimes in lieu of stops or semi-colons: where applicable, substitutions have been made. Dashes have been retained where they may signify pauses in delivery (perhaps to accommodate unspecified stage business, e.g. I.i. 15-17, where Hellena may pause, both for a response and to intensify Florinda's embarrassment; or I.ii.57, where Belvile may embrace Willmore), give emphasis to a final phrase (e.g. I.ii.151), indicate hesitation as a character thinks aloud (e.g. III.i.225), signal an abrupt change in addressee (e.g. I.i.56), or indicate an interrupted speech (e.g. III.i.242 and 244).

Q1's lineation is often idiosyncratic. Where the verse is very irregular and there is a precedent for setting it as prose in subsequent editions, this practice has been followed and changes from Q1 noted. Occasionally Q1 sets lines as prose when they could be verse and, again, adjustments have been made and changes noted. All editorial stage directions are in square brackets; others are as in Q1 (with standardised capitalisation), and changes in positioning are noted. Stage directions for entrances and exits in Q1 sometimes accommodate stage business involving other characters during the act of entering or exiting. These directions are retained, but occasional interventions have been necessary to clarify who is entering or exiting and who is merely involved in the accompanying stage actions. Speech prefixes have been written in full, though often abbreviated in Q1. Notes are supplied with the first use of a word or phrase. Subsequently, unless the context has changed, cross-references are made only from the first recurrence of the term in each act.

FURTHER READING

Aughterson, Kate, *Aphra Behn: the Comedies*, (Basingstoke, 2003)

Beach, Adam R., 'Carnival politics, generous satire, and nationalist spectacle in Behn's *The Rover*', *Eighteenth-Century Life*, 28 (2004), 1–19

Bender, Ashley B., 'Moving miniatures and circulating bodies in Aphra Behn's *The Rover*', *Restoration: Studies in English Literary Culture 1660–1700*, 31 (2007), 27–46

Carlson, Susan, 'Cannibalizing and carnivalizing: reviving Aphra Behn's *The Rover*', *Theatre Journal*, 47 (1995), 517–39

Caywood, Cynthia L., 'Deconstructing Aphras: Aphra Behn and her Biographers', *Restoration: Studies in English Literary Culture 1660–1700*, 24 (2000), 15–34

Copeland, Nancy, '"Once a whore and ever"? Whore and virgin in *The Rover* and its antecedents', *Restoration: Studies in English Literary Culture 1660–1700*, 16 (1992), 20–27

———, *Staging Gender in Behn and Centlivre: Women's Comedy and the Theatre* (Farnham, 2004)

Corse, Taylor, 'Seventeenth-century Naples and Aphra Behn's *The Rover*', *Restoration: Studies in English Literary Culture, 1660–1700*, 29 (2005), 41–51

De Ritter, J., 'The gypsy, the rover, and the wanderer: Aphra Behn's revision of Thomas Killigrew', *Restoration: Studies in English Literary Culture 1660–1700*, 10 (1986), 82–92

Diamond, Elin, 'Gestus and signature in Aphra Behn's *The Rover*', *ELH*, 56 (1) (1989), 519–41

Duchovnay, Gerald, 'Aphra Behn's religion', *Notes and Queries*, 221 (1976), 235–37

Duffy, Maureen, *The Passionate Shepherdess: Aphra Behn, 1640–89* (London, 1977, 2nd ed. 1989)

Engel, Laura, ed., *The Public's Open to Us All: Essays on Women and Performance in Eighteenth-century England* (Cambridge, 2009)

Franceschina, John, 'Shadow and substance in Aphra Behn's *The Rover*: the semiotics of Restoration performance', *Restoration: Studies in English Literary Culture 1660–1700*, 19 (1995), 29–42

Gallagher, Catherine, 'Who was that masked woman? The prostitute and the playwright in the comedies of Aphra Behn', *Women's Studies*, 15 (1988), 23–42

Gill, Catie, *Theatre and Culture in Early Modern England, 1650–1737* (Farnham, 2010)

Goreau, Angeline, *Reconstructing Aphra* (Oxford, 1980)

Hughes, Derek and Todd, Janet, eds., *The Cambridge Companion to Aphra Behn* (Cambridge, 2004)

Hughes, Derek, *The Theatre of Aphra Behn* (Basingstoke, 2001)

Hutner, Heidi, ed., *Rereading Aphra Behn: History, Theory, and Criticism* (Charlottesville and London, 1993)

Jones, Jane, 'New light on the background and early life of Aphra Behn', *Notes and Queries*, 235 (1990), 288–93

Kreis-Schinck, Annette, *Women, Writing, and the Theater in the Early Modern Period: the Plays of Aphra Behn and Susan Centlivre* (Madison, N.J., 2001)

Kroll, Richard, *Restoration Drama and 'The Circle of Commerce': Tragicomedy, Politics, and Trade in the Seventeenth Century* (Cambridge, 2011)

Link, Frederick, *Aphra Behn* (New York, 1968)

Lussier, Mark, '"The vile merchandize of Fortune": women, economy, and desire in Aphra Behn', *Women's Studies*, 18 (1991), 379–93

Mendelson, Sara Heller, 'Aphra Behn', in *The Mental World of Stuart Women: Three Studies* (Brighton, 1987)

Musser, Joseph F. Jr., '"Imposing nought but constancy in love": Aphra Behn snares the rover', *Restoration: Studies in English Literary Culture 1660–1700*, 3 (1979), 17–25

Nelson, Bonnie and Burroughs, Catherine, eds., *Teaching British Women Playwrights of the Restoration and Eighteenth Century* (New York, 2010)

O'Donnell, Mary Ann, *Aphra Behn: An Annotated Bibliography of Primary and Secondary Sources* (New York, 1986)

———, 'Tory wit and unconventional woman: Aphra Behn' in *Women Writers of the Seventeenth Century*, eds. Katharina M. Wilson & Frank J. Warnke (Athens, Ga., 1989), pp. 341–74

Owen, Susan J., ed., *A Companion to Restoration Drama* (Oxford, 2008)

Owens, W.R. and Goodman, L., eds., *Shakespeare, Aphra Behn and the Canon* (London, 1996)

Pacheco, Anita, 'Rape and the female subject in Aphra Behn's *The Rover*', *ELH*, 65 (2) (1998), 323–46

Pearson, Jacqueline, *The Prostituted Muse: Images of Women and Women Dramatists, 1642–1737* (New York, 1988)

Schafer, Elizabeth, 'Appropriating Aphra', *Australasian Drama Studies*, 19 (1991), 39–49

Spencer, Jane, *Aphra Behn's Afterlife* (Oxford, 2000)

Szilagyi, Stephen, 'The sexual politics of Behn's *Rover*: after patriarchy', *Studies in Philology*, 95 (4) (1998), 435–56
Taetzsch, Lynne, 'Romantic love replaces kinship exchange in Aphra Behn's Restoration drama', *Restoration: Studies in English Literary Culture 1660–1700*, 17 (1993), 30–38
Todd, Janet, *Aphra Behn* (Basingstoke, 1999)
———, *Aphra Behn Studies* (Cambridge, 1996)
———, *The Secret Life of Aphra Behn* (London, 1996)
———, ed., *The Works of Aphra Behn*, 7 vols. (London, 1992–96)
Weber, Harold, *The Restoration Rake-hero: Transformations in Sexual Understanding in Seventeenth-century England* (Madison, 1986)
Widmayer, Anne, 'Aphra Behn's *Rover* and Renaissance Balcony Scenes', *Theatre Annual: A Journal of Performance Studies*, 59 (2006), 63–86
Wiseman, S.J., *Aphra Behn* (Plymouth, 1996)

ABBREVIATIONS

B.L.	British Library
C	First collected edition, 1702
C2	Collected edition, 1724
It.	Italian
LTW	*The London Theatre World: 1660–1800*, ed. Robert D. Hume, Carbondale and Edwardsville, 1980
OED	*The Oxford English Dictionary*
om.	omitted
Q1	First Quarto, 1677
Q2	Second Quarto, 1697
Q3	Third Quarto, 1709
S	*The Works of Aphra Behn*, ed. Montague Summers, vol. 1, London, 1915
s.d.	stage direction
s.p.	speech prefix
T	*Oroonoko, The Rover and Other Works*, ed. Janet Todd, London, 1992
WPT	Women's Playhouse Trust

THE ROVER.

OR,

The Banish't Cavaliers.

As it is ACTED

AT

His Royal Highness

THE

Duke's Theatre.

Licensed *July* 2^d. 1677.

ROGER L'ESTRANGE.

LONDON,

Printed for *John Amery*, at the *Peacock*, against St. *Dunstan*'s Church in *Fleet-street*. 1677.

PROLOGUE

Wits, like physicians, never can agree,
When of a different society.
And Rabel's drops were never more cried down
By all the learned doctors of the town,
Than a new play whose author is unknown.
Nor can those doctors with more malice sue
(And powerful purses) the dissenting few,
Than those, with an insulting pride, do rail
At all who are not of their own cabal.
   If a young poet hit your humour right,
You judge him then out of revenge and spite.
So amongst men there are ridiculous elves,
Who monkeys hate for being too like themselves.
So that the reason of the grand debate
Why wit so oft is damned when good plays take,
Is that you censure as you love, or hate.
   Thus like a learned conclave poets sit,
Catholic judges both of sense and wit,
And damn or save, as they themselves think fit.
Yet those who to others' faults are so severe,
Are not so perfect but themselves may err.
Some write correct, indeed, but then the whole
(Bating their own dull stuff i'th' play) is stole:
As bees do suck from flowers their honey dew,
So they rob others striving to please you.
   Some write their characters genteel and fine,
But then they do so toil for every line,
That what to you does easy seem, and plain,
Is the hard issue of their labouring brain.
And some, th'effects of all their pains we see,

3 *Rabel's drops* a patent medicine.
9 *cabal* secret or private clique.
12 *men* Q1, Q2, C, C2 (them Q3).
elves malicious persons.
18 *and wit* Q1, Q3, C, C2 (of wit Q2).
21 *themselves* Q1, Q3, C2 (they themselves Q2, C).
23 *bating* excepting

Is but to mimic good extempore.
Others, by long converse about the town,
Have wit enough to write a lewd lampoon,
But their chief skill lies in a bawdy song.
In short, the only wit that's now in fashion
Is but the gleanings of good conversation.
As for the author of this coming play,
I asked him what he thought fit I should say
In thanks for your good company today:
He called me fool, and said it was well known
You came not here for our sakes, but your own.
New plays are stuffed with wits, and with debauches,
That crowd and sweat like cits in May-Day coaches.

WRITTEN BY A PERSON OF QUALITY

42 *debauches* ed. (deboches Q1).
43 *cits* citizens, ordinary people

THE PERSONS OF THE PLAY

DON ANTONIO, *the viceroy's son*
DON PEDRO, *a noble Spaniard, his friend*
FLORINDA, *sister to Don Pedro*
HELLENA, *a gay young woman, designed for a nun, and sister to Florinda*
BELVILE, *an English colonel in love with Florinda*
WILLMORE, *the Rover*
ANGELLICA BIANCA, *a famous courtesan*
MORETTA, *her woman*
BLUNT, *an English country gentleman*
FREDERICK, *an English gentleman, and friend to Belvile and Blunt*
VALERIA, *a kinswoman to Florinda*
CALLIS, *governess to Florinda and Hellena*
LUCETTA, *a jilting wench*
STEPHANO, *servant to Don Pedro*
PHILIPPO, *Lucetta's gallant*
SANCHO, *pimp to Lucetta*
BISKEY *and* SEBASTIAN, *two bravos to Angellica*
PAGE *to Don Antonio*
Officers and soldiers
Servants; other masqueraders (men and women)

THE SCENE, *Naples in carnival time*

10 Blunt Q2, C, C2 (Fred. Q1, Q3).
Sexes segregated in Q1. See the list of 'The Actors' Names', p. 6.

The Actors Names.

Mr. *Jevorne*,	*Don Antonio*,	The Vice-Roy's Son.
Mr. *Medburne*,	*Don Pedro*,	A Noble *Spaniard*, his Friend.
Mr. *Betterton*,	*Belvile*,	An *English* Colonel in Love with *Florinda*.
Mr. *Smith*,	*Willmore*,	The *ROVER*.
Mr. *Crosbie*,	*Frederick*,	An *English* Gentleman, and Friend to *Bel.* and *Fred.*
Mr. *Underhill*,	*Blunt*,	An *English* Country Gentleman.
Mr. *Richards*,	*Stephano*,	Servant to *Don Pedro*.
Mr. *Percivall*,	*Philippo*,	*Lucetta*'s Gallant.
Mr. *John Lee*,	*Sancho*,	Pimp to *Lucetta*.
	Biskey, and *Sebastian*,	*Two Bravo's to* Angellica.
	Officers and Souldiers.	
	Page	To *Don Antonio*.

Women.

Mrs. *Betterton*,	*Florinda*.	Sister to *Don Pedro*.
Mrs. *Barrer*,	*Hellena*,	A gay Young Woman design'd for a Nun, and Sister to *Florinda*.
Mrs. *Hughs*,	*Valeria*,	A Kinswoman to *Florinda*.
Mrs. *Gwin*,	*Angellica Bianca*,	A Famous Courtizan.
Mrs. *Leigh*,	*Moretta*,	Her Woman.
Mrs. *Norris*,	*Callis*,	Governess to *Florinda* and *Hellena*.
Mrs. *Gillo*,	*Lucetta*,	A Jilting Wench.

Servants, Other *Masqueraders* Men and Women.

The Scene *NAPLES*, in Carnival time.

ACT I, SCENE i

A chamber

Enter FLORINDA *and* HELLENA

FLORINDA

What an impertinent thing is a young girl bred in a nunnery! How full of questions! Prithee no more, Hellena; I have told thee more than thou understand'st already.

HELLENA

The more's my grief. I would fain know as much as you, which makes me so inquisitive; nor is't enough I know you're a lover, unless you tell me, too, who 'tis you sigh for.

FLORINDA

When you're a lover I'll think you fit for a secret of that nature.

HELLENA

'Tis true, I never was a lover yet – but I begin to have a shrewd guess what 'tis to be so, and fancy it very pretty to sigh, and sing, and blush, and wish, and dream and wish, and long and wish to see the man; and when I do, look pale and tremble, just as you did when my brother brought home the fine English colonel to see you – what do you call him, Don Belvile?

FLORINDA

Fie, Hellena.

HELLENA

That blush betrays you. I am sure 'tis so – or is it Don Antonio the viceroy's son? – Or perhaps the rich old Don Vincentio, whom my father designs you for a husband? – Why do you blush again?

FLORINDA

With indignation; and how near soever my father thinks I am

0 s.d. 1 *chamber* private room rather than bedroom.
2 *Prithee* [I] pray thee.
4 *fain* gladly, willingly.
5 *I know* Q1 (to know Q2).
16 *viceroy* vice-king, one governing in the name and by the authority of the supreme ruler.
17 *designs you for a* Q1, Q3 (designs for your Q2).
designs designates, intends.

to marrying that hated object, I shall let him see I understand better what's due to my beauty, birth, and fortune, and more – to my soul, than to obey those unjust commands.

HELLENA

Now hang me if I don't love thee for that dear disobedience. I love mischief strangely, as most of our sex do, who are come to love nothing else – but tell me, dear Florinda, don't you love that fine *Anglese*? For I vow, next to loving him myself, 'twill please me most that you do so, for he is so gay and so handsome!

FLORINDA

Hellena, a maid designed for a nun ought not to be so curious in a discourse of love.

HELLENA

And dost thou think that ever I'll be a nun? Or at least till I'm so old, I'm fit for nothing else? Faith, no, sister; and that which makes me long to know whether you love Belvile, is because I hope he has some mad companion or other that will spoil my devotion. Nay, I'm resolved to provide myself this carnival, if there be e'er a handsome proper fellow of my humour above ground, though I ask first.

FLORINDA

Prithee be not so wild.

HELLENA

Now you have provided yourself of a man, you take no care for poor me. Prithee tell me, what dost thou see about me that is unfit for love? Have I not a world of youth? A humour gay?

20–2 *see I understand . . . and more – to* ed. (see, I understand . . . and more to Q1).
24 *strangely* very greatly.
26 *Anglese* Englishman (a hybrid word, combining the French 'Anglais' with the Italian 'Inglese').
27 *gay* exuberantly cheerful.
29 *designed* intended.
34 *spoil* make spoil of, i.e. plunder her devotion for himself.
35 *provide* furnish, equip.
carnival from the Italian 'carne levare': the putting away of flesh as food (*OED*); festivity prior to the forty days of Lent when Catholics abstained from eating meat, characterised by freedom from social restrictions and the indulgence of the body.
36 *proper* 1) fine 2) honest, respectable.
humour disposition.
37 *though . . . first* even if I have to take the initiative.
39 *of a man* Q1 (with a man Q2).

A beauty passable? A vigour desirable? Well shaped? Clean limbed? Sweet breathed? And sense enough to know how all these ought to be employed to the best advantage? Yes, I do and will. Therefore lay aside your hopes of my fortune by my being a devotee, and tell me how you came acquainted with this Belvile; for I perceive you knew him before he came to Naples.

FLORINDA

Yes, I knew him at the siege of Pamplona; he was then a colonel of French horse, who when the town was ransacked, nobly treated my brother and myself, preserving us from all insolences; and I must own, besides great obligations, I have I know not what that pleads kindly for him about my heart, and will suffer no other to enter. – But see, my brother.

Enter DON PEDRO [*and*] STEPHANO, *with a masquing habit, and* CALLIS

PEDRO

Good morrow, sister. Pray, when saw you your lover Don Vincentio?

FLORINDA

I know not, sir. – Callis, when was he here? For I consider it so little, I know not when it was.

PEDRO

I have a command from my father here, to tell you you ought not to despise him, a man of so vast a fortune, and such a passion for you. – Stephano, my things.

Puts on his masquing habit

FLORINDA

A passion for me! 'Tis more than e'er I saw, or he had a desire should be known. I hate Vincentio, sir, and I would not have a man so dear to me as my brother follow the ill customs of our

46 *devotee* ed. (devote Q1) a religious zealot, a nun – with, perhaps, a mischievous allusion to the practice of using religious vocabulary for the erotic in the language of French courtly love.

48 *Pamplona* ed. (Pampulona Q1) the strongly fortified capital of Navarre.

49 *horse* cavalry. He is an exile, hired for foreign service.

53 s.d. 1 *masquing habit* set of clothes for a masquerade; i.e. an elaborate mask and disguise.

54 *lover* suitor.

58 *father here, . . . you you ought* ed. (Father here . . . you, you ought Q1).

60 *my things* Q1 (m'thinks – Q2).

country and make a slave of his sister. – And sir, my father's will, I'm sure you may divert.

PEDRO

I know not how dear I am to you, but I wish only to be ranked in your esteem, equal with the English Colonel Belvile. Why do you frown and blush? Is there any guilt belongs to the name of that cavalier?

FLORINDA

I'll not deny I value Belvile: when I was exposed to such dangers as the licensed lust of common soldiers threatened when rage and conquest flew through the city – then Belvile, this criminal for my sake, threw himself into all dangers to save my honour – and will you not allow him my esteem?

PEDRO

Yes, pay him what you will in honour – but you must consider Don Vincentio's fortune, and the jointure he'll make you.

FLORINDA

Let him consider my youth, beauty, and fortune; which ought not to be thrown away on his age and jointure.

PEDRO

'Tis true, he's not so young and fine a gentleman as that Belvile – but what jewels will that cavalier present you with? Those of his eyes and heart?

HELLENA

And are not those better than any Don Vincentio has brought from the Indies?

PEDRO

Why how now! Has your nunnery-breeding taught you to understand the value of hearts and eyes?

HELLENA

Better than to believe Vincentio's deserve value from any woman. He may perhaps increase her bags, but not her family.

69 *cavalier* 1) horse-soldier 2) one who fought for Charles I against Parliament.
70–1 *such dangers . . . threatened* sexual violation of women traditionally allowed to the victors.
72–3 *criminal . . . sake* Belvile took Florinda's side against his own men.
73 *threw* Q3 (through Q1).
76 *jointure* estate settled on a wife, to be enjoyed by her after her husband's death.
87 *bags* money bags, with a jibe at Vincentio's supposed lack of virility ('to bag' could also mean 'to make pregnant').

PEDRO

This is fine! Go – up to your devotion. You are not designed for the conversation of lovers.

HELLENA (*Aside*)

Nor saints, yet a while, I hope. [*To* PEDRO] – Is't not enough you make a nun of me, but you must cast my sister away too, exposing her to a worse confinement than a religious life?

PEDRO

The girl's mad. It is a confinement to be carried into the country, to an ancient villa belonging to the family of the Vincentios these five hundred years, and have no other prospect than that pleasing one of seeing all her own that meets her eyes – a fine air, large fields and gardens, where she may walk and gather flowers!

HELLENA

When, by moon-light? For I am sure she dares not encounter with the heat of the sun; that were a task only for Don Vincentio and his Indian breeding, who loves it in the dog-days. And if these be her daily divertissements, what are those of the night? To lie in a wide moth-eaten bed-chamber with furniture in fashion in the reign of King Sancho the First; the bed, that which his forefathers lived and died in.

PEDRO

Very well.

HELLENA

This apartment – new furbished and fitted out for the young wife – he, out of freedom, makes his dressing room; and being a frugal and a jealous coxcomb, instead of a valet to uncase his feeble carcass, he desires you to do that office – signs of favour, I'll assure you, and such as you must not hope for, unless your woman be out of the way.

PEDRO

Have you done yet?

88 *fine! Go – up* ed. (fine – go – up Q1).
93 *it is* Q1 (is it Q3).
95–6 *prospect* 1) view 2) expectation.
101–2 *dog-days* the days when the Dog-star rises (traditionally the hottest and most unwholesome time of the year, associated with malignant influences).
102 *divertissements* entertainments.
104 *King Sancho the First* Sancho I Garces, King of Navarre (Pamplona) from 905.
107 *furbished* ed. (furbrusht Q1) renovated.
109 *coxcomb* fool. *uncase* undress.

HELLENA

That honour being past, the giant stretches himself, yawns and sighs a belch or two, loud as a musket – throws himself into bed, and expects you in his foul sheets, and e'er you can get yourself undressed, calls you with a snore or two – and are not these fine blessings to a young lady?

PEDRO

Have you done yet?

HELLENA

And this man you must kiss, nay you must kiss none but him, too – and nuzzle through his beard to find his lips – and this you must submit to for threescore years, and all for a jointure.

PEDRO

For all your character of Don Vincentio, she is as like to marry him as she was before.

HELLENA

Marry Don Vincentio! Hang me, such a wedlock would be worse than adultery with another man. I had rather see her in the *Hostel de Dieu*, to waste her youth there in vows and be a handmaid to lazars and cripples, than to lose it in such a marriage.

PEDRO

You have considered, sister, that Belvile has no fortune to bring to you, banished his country, despised at home, and pitied abroad?

HELLENA

What then? The viceroy's son is better than that old Sir Fisty. Don Vincentio! Don Indian! He thinks he's trading to Gambo still, and would barter himself – that bell and bauble – for your youth and fortune.

114 *himself* Q3 (itself Q1) 115 *loud* Q1 (as loud C).

123 *character . . . Vincentio* description of Don Vincentio's qualities.

127 *Hostel de Dieu* (usually medieval) hospital run by a religious order.

128 *lazars* poor and diseased people, especially lepers.

131 *to you* ed. (you to Q1).

133 *Sir Fisty* Q1 is unclear; this may read 'Fisty' or 'Fifty' (Fifty Q3; Fisty C; unclear C2). If 'Fifty', Hellena is making a tame jibe at Vincentio's age; if 'Fisty', it is a play on 'fist' (v2 *OED*), meaning 'to break wind'.

134 *Gambo* Gambia, West Africa, supplying less exotic trading opportunities than the Gold Coast, further south. The West-African slave trade began to boom in the middle of the seventeenth century.

135 *bell and bauble* trifle (like the worthless objects offered to indigenous peoples by some European traders in return for items of great value).

PEDRO

Callis, take her hence, and lock her up all this carnival, and at Lent she shall begin her everlasting penance in a monastery.

HELLENA

I care not. I had rather be a nun than be obliged to marry as you would have me, if I were designed for't.

PEDRO

Do not fear the blessing of that choice. You shall be a nun.

HELLENA (*Aside*)

Shall I so? You may chance to be mistaken in my way of devotion – a nun! Yes, I am like to make a fine nun! I have an excellent humour for a grate. No, I'll have a saint of my own to pray to shortly, if I like any that dares venture on me.

PEDRO

Callis, make it your business to watch this wild cat. As for you, Florinda, I've only tried you all this while and urged my father's will – but mine is, that you would love Antonio; he is brave and young, and all that can complete the happiness of a gallant maid. This absence of my father will give us opportunity to free you from Vincentio by marrying here, which you must do tomorrow.

FLORINDA

Tomorrow!

PEDRO

Tomorrow, or 'twill be too late – 'tis not my friendship to Antonio which makes me urge this, but love to thee and hatred to Vincentio – therefore resolve upon tomorrow.

FLORINDA

Sir, I shall strive to do as shall become your sister.

PEDRO

I'll both believe and trust you. Adieu.

Exeunt PEDRO *and* STEPHANO

HELLENA

As becomes his sister! That is to be as resolved your way as he is his.

HELLENA *goes to* CALLIS

138 *Lent* in the Christian church, a time of penance in preparation for Easter. See Breughel's painting *The Battle of Carnival and Lent.*

144 *grate* a framework of bars fixed in a door or window to allow restricted communication.

147 *tried* tested.

FLORINDA

I ne'er till now perceived my ruin near.
I've no defence against Antonio's love,
For he has all the advantages of nature,
The moving arguments of youth and fortune.

HELLENA

But hark you, Callis, you will not be so cruel to lock me up indeed, will you?

CALLIS

I must obey the commands I have. Besides, do you consider what a life you are going to lead?

HELLENA

Yes, Callis, that of a nun: and till then I'll be indebted a world of prayers to you if you'll let me now see what I never did, the divertissements of a carnival.

CALLIS

What, go in masquerade? 'Twill be a fine farewell to the world, I take it. Pray what would you do there?

HELLENA

That which all the world does, as I am told – be as mad as the rest and take all innocent freedoms. – Sister, you'll go too, will you not? Come prithee be not sad. We'll outwit twenty brothers if you'll be ruled by me. Come put off this dull humour with your clothes, and assume one as gay, and as fantastic as the dress my cousin Valeria and I have provided, and let's ramble.

FLORINDA

Callis, will you give us leave to go?

CALLIS (*Aside*)

I have a youthful itch of going myself.
– Madam, if I thought your brother might not know it, and I might wait on you; for, by my troth, I'll not trust young girls alone.

FLORINDA

Thou see'st my brother's gone already, and thou shalt attend and watch us.

Enter STEPHANO

167 *have* Q1, Q3 (hate Q2, C, C2).
179 *ramble* roam in a free and unrestrained fashion (with sexual resonances of libertine behaviour).

STEPHANO

Madam, the habits are come, and your cousin Valeria is dressed and stays for you.

FLORINDA

'Tis well. I'll write a note, and if I chance to see Belvile and want an opportunity to speak to him, that shall let him know what I've resolved in favour of him.

HELLENA

Come, let's in and dress us.

Exeunt

[ACT I,] SCENE ii

A long street

Enter BELVILE, *melancholy,* BLUNT *and* FREDERICK

FREDERICK

Why, what the devil ails the colonel in a time when all the world is gay, to look like mere Lent thus? Hadst thou been long enough in Naples to have been in love, I should have sworn some such judgement had befallen thee.

BELVILE

No, I have made no new amours since I came to Naples.

FREDERICK

You have left none behind you in Paris?

BELVILE

Neither.

FREDERICK

I cannot divine the cause then, unless the old cause, the want of money.

187 *Madam,* Q3 (Mad? Q1).
habits costumes.
188 *stays* waits.

1 *Why, . . . colonel in* ed. (Whe what . . . Devil ails the Coll. In Q1) The exclamation 'whe' occurs frequently in Q1 and has been emended to 'why' throughout. Todd notes that 'whe' 'suggests a stronger tone than "why" possesses' (T, p. 364).
5 *amours* romantic liaisons.
8 *want* lack.

BLUNT

And another old cause, the want of a wench. Would not that revive you?

BELVILE

You are mistaken, Ned.

BLUNT

Nay, 'sheartlikins, then thou'rt past cure.

FREDERICK

I have found it out: thou hast renewed thy acquaintance with the lady that cost thee so many sighs at the siege of Pamplona. – Pox on't, what d'e you call her – her brother's a noble Spaniard, nephew to the dead general. – Florinda! Ay, Florinda. And will nothing serve thy turn but that damned virtuous woman, whom on my conscience thou lov'st in spite too, because thou seest little or no possibility of gaining her?

BELVILE

Thou art mistaken; I have int'rest enough in that lovely virgin's heart to make me proud and vain, were it not abated by the severity of a brother, who perceiving my happiness –

FREDERICK

Has civilly forbid thee the house?

BELVILE

'Tis so, to make way for a powerful rival, the viceroy's son, who has the advantage of me in being a man of fortune, a Spaniard, and her brother's friend; which gives him liberty to make his court, whilst I have recourse only to letters, and distant looks
from her window, which are as soft and kind
As those which Heaven sends down on penitents.

BLUNT

Heyday! 'Sheartlikins, simile! By this light the man is quite spoiled. – Fred, what the devil are we made of, that we cannot be thus concerned for a wench? 'Sheartlikins, our Cupids are

13 *'sheartlikins* from ''adsheartlikins'. 'Ads' is a variant of 'ods', a minced form of 'God's'; 'heartlikin', or 'little heart', is a term of endearment: the expression becomes characteristic of Blunt.

21–2 *int'rest . . . heart* stake (share) . . . affections.

27–8 *liberty . . . court* freedom to carry out his courtship openly.

30 *As . . . penitents* Q1 changes from prose to verse here.

32–3 *– Fred . . . wench?* ed. (– *Fred. . . .* Wench – Q1) *'Fred.'* may be a speech prefix in Q1, but the lines are set within Blunt's speech. The dash after 'Wench' indicates that a further speech prefix for Blunt may have been accidentally omitted.

like the cooks of the camp – they can roast or boil a woman, but they have none of the fine tricks to set 'em off – no hogoes to make the sauce pleasant, and the stomach sharp.

FREDERICK

I dare swear I have had a hundred as young, kind, and handsome as this Florinda; and dogs eat me, if they were not as troublesome to me i'th' morning as they were welcome o'er night.

BLUNT

And yet, I warrant, he would not touch another woman, if he might have her for nothing.

BELVILE

That's thy joy, a cheap whore.

BLUNT

Why, 'sheartlikins, I love a frank soul. When did you ever hear of an honest woman that took a man's money? I warrant 'em good ones. But gentlemen, you may be free; you have been kept so poor with parliaments and protectors, that the little stock you have is not worth preserving – but I thank my stars I had more grace than to forfeit my estate by cavaliering.

BELVILE

Methinks only following the court should be sufficient to entitle 'em to that.

BLUNT

'Sheartlikins, they know I follow it to do it no good, unless they pick a hole in my coat for lending you money now and then; which is a greater crime to my conscience, gentlemen, than to the Commonwealth.

Enter WILLMORE

WILLMORE

Ha! Dear Belvile! Noble colonel!

BELVILE

Willmore! Welcome ashore, my dear rover! – What happy wind blew us this good fortune?

35 *hogoes* piquant flavours and relishes.

44 *Why,* ed. (Whe I Q1).

47 *parliaments and protectors* Since the imprisonment and beheading of Charles I in 1649, Britain was governed by Parliament, after 1653 under the leadership of Protectors, Oliver and Richard Cromwell, who confiscated many Royalist estates.

53 *pick a hole in my coat* find fault with me.

55 *Commonwealth* the republican government, 1649–60.

WILLMORE

Let me salute my dear Fred, and then command me. – How is't, honest lad?

FREDERICK

Faith, sir, the old compliment: infinitely the better to see my dear mad Willmore again. Prithee why camest thou ashore? And where's the prince?

WILLMORE

He's well and reigns still Lord of the Wat'ry Element. I must aboard again within a day or two, and my business ashore was only to enjoy myself a little this carnival.

BELVILE

Pray know our new friend, sir; he's but bashful, a raw traveller, but honest, stout, and one of us.

Embraces BLUNT

WILLMORE

That you esteem him gives him an int'rest here.

BLUNT

Your servant, sir.

WILLMORE

But well – faith I'm glad to meet you again in a warm climate, where the kind sun has its god-like power still over the wine and women. Love and mirth are my business in Naples! And if I mistake not the place, here's an excellent market for chapmen of my humour.

BELVILE

See, here be those kind merchants of love you look for.

Enter several men in masquing habits, some playing on music, others dancing after; women dressed like courtesans, with papers pinned on their breasts, and baskets of flowers in their hands

BLUNT

'Sheartlikins, what have we here!

FREDERICK

Now the game begins.

63 *prince* the exiled son of Charles I, future Charles II.
74 *chapmen* itinerant dealers who buy and sell, or purchasers (as here).
76 s.d. 1 *masquing habits* See I.i.53 s.d. note.
s.d. 2 *music* musical instruments.

WILLMORE

Fine pretty creatures! May a stranger have leave to look and love? – What's here? (*Reads the papers*) – 'Roses for every month'!

BLUNT

'Roses for every month'! What means that?

BELVILE

They are, or would have you think they're courtesans, who here in Naples are to be hired by the month.

WILLMORE

Kind and obliging to inform us – pray where do these roses grow? I would fain plant some of 'em in a bed of mine.

WOMAN

Beware such roses, sir.

WILLMORE

A pox of fear: I'll be baked with thee between a pair of sheets, and that's thy proper still; so I might but strew such roses over me and under me. Fair one, would you would give me leave to gather at your bush this idle month; I would go near to make somebody smell of it all the year after.

BELVILE

And thou hast need of such a remedy, for thou stink'st of tar and ropes' ends like a dock or pesthouse.

The woman puts herself into the hands of a man and exeunt

WILLMORE

Nay, nay, you shall not leave me so.

BELVILE

By all means use no violence here.

WILLMORE

Death! Just as I was going to be damnably in love, to have her led off! I could pluck that rose out of his hand, and even kiss the bed the bush grew in.

80 s.d. *Reads . . . papers* follows line in Q1.

84 *Kind . . . obliging* i.e. be so good as.

87–91 *I'll . . . after.* In distillation, the substance to be distilled is subjected to heat: he is implying that the best kind of still is a pair of sheets containing roses like her, with whom he would willingly be distilled into a strong perfume.

93 *dock* originally where vessels were built or brought for repair.
pesthouse hospital for plague (pestilence) sufferers.

94–5 The implication is that Willmore offers force – either to the woman, to pull her to him, or to the man, by being about to draw his sword.

FREDERICK

No friend to love like a long voyage at sea.

BLUNT

Except a nunnery, Fred.

WILLMORE

Death! But will they not be kind? Quickly be kind? Thou know'st I'm no tame sigher, but a rampant lion of the forest.

Advance from the farther end of the scenes, two men dressed all over with horns of several sorts, making grimaces at one another, with papers pinned on their backs

BELVILE

Oh the fantastical rogues, how they're dressed! 'Tis a satire against the whole sex.

WILLMORE

Is this a fruit that grows in this warm country?

BELVILE

Yes, 'tis pretty to see these Italians start, swell, and stab at the word 'cuckold', and yet stumble at horns on every threshold.

WILLMORE

See what's on their back. (*Reads*) 'Flowers of every night.' Ah, rogue! And more sweet than roses of every month! This is a gardener of Adam's own breeding.

They dance

BELVILE

What think you of those grave people? Is a wake in Essex half so mad or extravagant?

WILLMORE

I like their sober grave way; 'tis a kind of legal authorised fornication, where the men are not chid for't, nor the women despised, as amongst our dull English. Even the monsieurs want that part of good manners.

BELVILE

But here in Italy, a monsieur is the humblest best-bred gentle-

102 s.d. 1 *Advance* ed. (Advances Q1).
the farther end of the scenes i.e. up stage.

107 *horns* Traditionally it was supposed that horns grew on the forehead of a man with an unfaithful wife. As the traditional sign of cuckoldry, horns are the basis of many jokes in English comedy from Shakespeare onwards.

111 *Essex* Blunt's home ground (see II.i.40 and 79).

115 *monsieurs* Frenchmen.

man – duels are so baffled by bravos that an age shows not one but between a Frenchman and a hangman, who is as much too hard for him on the Piazza as they are for a Dutchman on the New Bridge. But see, another crew.

Enter FLORINDA, HELLENA, *and* VALERIA, *dressed like gipsies;* CALLIS *and* STEPHANO, LUCETTA, PHILIPPO *and* SANCHO *in masquerade*

HELLENA

Sister, there's your Englishman, and with him a handsome proper fellow. I'll to him, and instead of telling him his fortune, try my own.

WILLMORE

Gipsies, on my life. Sure these will prattle if a man cross their hands. (*Goes to* HELLENA) – Dear, pretty, and, I hope, young devil, will you tell an amorous stranger what luck he's like to have?

HELLENA

Have a care how you venture with me, sir, lest I pick your pocket, which will more vex your English humour than an Italian fortune will please you.

WILLMORE

How the devil cam'st thou to know my country and humour?

HELLENA

The first I guess by a certain forward impudence, which does not displease me at this time; and the loss of your money will vex you because I hope you have but very little to lose.

WILLMORE

Egad, child, thou'rt i'th' right; it is so little I dare not offer it thee for a kindness. But cannot you divine what other things of more value I have about me that I would more willingly part with?

118 *baffled* confounded, foiled.
bravos hired ruffians, assassins.
120 *Piazza* large open square.
they the French, who were successful in Flanders (see also II.i.253 note).
121 s.d. 1–2 *dressed like gipsies* so that their faces are hidden by veils or head-dresses. See Willmore's comments at ll. 125–8, 229–300, and the exchange at 173–6.
125–6 *cross their hands* i.e. with silver; put money in their hands.
130 *humour* temperament.
136 *Egad* by God!

HELLENA

Indeed no, that's the business of a witch, and I am but a gipsy yet. Yet without looking in your hand, I have a parlous guess 'tis some foolish heart you mean, an inconstant English heart, as little worth stealing as your purse.

WILLMORE

Nay, then thou dost deal with the devil, that's certain. Thou hast guessed as right as if thou hadst been one of that number it has languished for. I find you'll be better acquainted with it, nor can you take it in a better time; for I am come from sea, child, and Venus not being propitious to me in her own element, I have a world of love in store. Would you would be good-natured and take some on't off my hands.

HELLENA

Why, I could be inclined that way, but for a foolish vow I am going to make – to die a maid.

WILLMORE

Then thou art damned without redemption, and as I am a good Christian, I ought in charity to divert so wicked a design. Therefore prithee, dear creature, let me know quickly when and where I shall begin to set a helping hand to so good a work.

HELLENA

If you should prevail with my tender heart – as I begin to fear you will, for you have horrible loving eyes – there will be difficulty in't, that you'll hardly undergo for my sake.

WILLMORE

Faith, child, I have been bred in dangers, and wear a sword that has been employed in a worse cause than for a handsome kind woman. Name the danger; let it be anything but a long siege, and I'll undertake it.

HELLENA

Can you storm?

WILLMORE

Oh, most furiously.

HELLENA

What think you of a nunnery wall? For he that wins me must gain that first.

140 *parlous* clever.
147 *Venus . . . element* The goddess of love came from the sea.
151 *maid* virgin.
163 *storm* violently assault a fortified place.

WILLMORE

A nun! Oh, how I love thee for't! There's no sinner like a young saint. Nay, now there's no denying me; the old law had no curse – to a woman – like dying a maid: witness Jephthah's daughter.

HELLENA

A very good text this, if well handled; and I perceive, Father Captain, you would impose no severe penance on her who were inclined to console herself before she took orders.

WILLMORE

If she be young and handsome.

HELLENA

Ay, there's it. But if she be not –

WILLMORE

By this hand, child, I have an implicit faith, and dare venture on thee with all faults. Besides, 'tis more meritorious to leave the world when thou hast tasted and proved the pleasure on't. Then 'twill be a virtue in thee, which now will be pure ignorance.

HELLENA

I perceive, good Father Captain, you design only to make me fit for Heaven. But if, on the contrary, you should quite divert me from it, and bring me back to the world again, I should have a new man to seek, I find. And what a grief that will be – for when I begin, I fancy I shall love like anything; I never tried yet.

WILLMORE

Egad, and that's kind! – Prithee, dear creature, give me credit for a heart, for faith, I'm a very honest fellow. Oh, I long to come first to the banquet of love! And such a swinging appetite I bring. Oh, I'm impatient. Thy lodging, sweetheart, thy lodging, or I'm a dead man!

HELLENA

Why must we be either guilty of fornication or murder if we converse with you men? And is there no difference between leave to love me, and leave to lie with me?

WILLMORE

Faith, child, they were made to go together.

169 *Jephthah's daughter* Judges 11: 37–40: Jephthah sacrificed his daughter to keep a promise and for four days before being killed she was allowed to roam and bemoan her virginity.

170–1 *Father Captain* alluding to Willmore's mock-adoption of a religious argument.

172 *orders* final vows to make her a nun.

183 *anything; I* ed. (anything, I Q1).

186 *swinging* fine, splendid.

LUCETTA (*Pointing to* BLUNT)

Are you sure this is the man?

SANCHO

When did I mistake your game?

LUCETTA

This is a stranger, I know by his gazing; if he be brisk he'll venture to follow me, and then, if I understand my trade, he's mine. He's English too, and they say that's a sort of good-natured loving people, and have generally so kind an opinion of themselves that a woman with any wit may flatter 'em into any sort of fool she pleases.

She often passes by BLUNT *and gazes on him; he struts and cocks, and walks and gazes on her*

BLUNT

'Tis so, she is taken – I have beauties which my false glass at home did not discover.

FLORINDA (*Aside*)

This woman watches me so, I shall get no opportunity to discover myself to him, and so miss the intent of my coming. [*To* BELVILE] (*Looking in his hand*) – But as I was saying, sir – by this line you should be a lover.

BELVILE

I thought how right you guessed: all men are in love, or pretend to be so. Come, let me go; I'm weary of this fooling.

Walks away

FLORINDA

I will not till you have confessed whether the passion that you have vowed Florinda be true or false.

She holds him; he strives to get from her

BELVILE (*Turns quick towards her*)

Florinda!

FLORINDA

Softly.

193 This is the first of several switches in focus on stage which occur throughout this scene.
194 *game* prey.
201 *glass* looking-glass.
202 *discover* reveal.

BELVILE
Thou hast named one will fix me here forever.

FLORINDA
She'll be disappointed then, who expects you this night at the garden gate. And if you fail not, as – (*Looks on* CALLIS, *who observes 'em*) let me see the other hand – you will go near to do, she vows to die or make you happy.

BELVILE
What canst thou mean?

FLORINDA
That which I say. Farewell.

Offers to go

BELVILE
Oh charming sybil, stay; complete that joy which as it is will turn into distraction! Where must I be? At the garden gate? I know it. At night, you say? I'll sooner forfeit Heaven than disobey.

Enter DON PEDRO *and other maskers, and pass over the stage*

CALLIS
Madam, your brother's here.

FLORINDA
Take this to instruct you farther.

Gives him a letter, and goes off

FREDERICK
Have a care, sir, what you promise; this may be a trap laid by her brother to ruin you.

BELVILE
Do not disturb my happiness with doubts.

Opens the letter

WILLMORE [*To* HELLENA]
My dear pretty creature, a thousand blessings on thee! Still in this habit, you say? And after dinner at this place?

HELLENA
Yes, if you will swear to keep your heart and not bestow it between this and that.

215–16 s.d. *Looks . . . 'em* follows speech Q1.
230 *habit* outfit.

WILLMORE

By all the little gods of love, I swear; I'll leave it with you, and if you run away with it, those deities of justice will revenge me.

Exeunt all the women [*except* LUCETTA]

FREDERICK

Do you know the hand?

BELVILE

'Tis Florinda's.

All blessings fall upon the virtuous maid.

FREDERICK

Nay, no idolatry; a sober sacrifice I'll allow you.

BELVILE

Oh friends, the welcom'st news! The softest letter! – Nay, you shall all see it! And could you now be serious, I might be made the happiest man the sun shines on!

WILLMORE

The reason of this mighty joy?

BELVILE

See how kindly she invites me to deliver her from the threatened violence of her brother. Will you not assist me?

WILLMORE

I know not what thou mean'st, but I'll make one at any mischief where a woman's concerned. But she'll be grateful to us for the favour, will she not?

BELVILE

How mean you?

WILLMORE

How should I mean? Thou know'st there's but one way for a woman to oblige me.

BELVILE

Do not profane – the maid is nicely virtuous.

WILLMORE

Who, pox, then she's fit for nothing but a husband. Let her e'en go, colonel.

FREDERICK

Peace, she's the colonel's mistress, sir.

WILLMORE

Let her be the devil; if she be thy mistress, I'll serve her. Name the way.

251 *nicely* scrupulously.

BELVILE

Read here this postscript.

Gives him a letter

WILLMORE (*Reads*)

'At ten at night – at the garden gate, of which, if I cannot get the key, I will contrive a way over the wall – come attended with a friend or two.' – Kind heart, if we three cannot weave a string to let her down a garden wall, 'twere pity but the hangman wove one for us all.

FREDERICK

Let her alone for that; your woman's wit, your fair kind woman, will out-trick a broker or a Jew, and contrive like a Jesuit in chains. – But see, Ned Blunt is stolen out after the lure of a damsel.

Exeunt BLUNT *and* LUCETTA

BELVILE

So, he'll scarce find his way home again unless we get him cried by the bellman in the market place. And 'twould sound prettily – a lost English boy of thirty.

FREDERICK

I hope 'tis some common crafty sinner, one that will fit him. It may be she'll sell him for Peru: the rogue's sturdy, and would work well in a mine. At least I hope she'll dress him for our mirth, cheat him of all, then have him well-favouredly banged, and turned out naked at midnight.

WILLMORE

Prithee what humour is he of, that you wish him so well?

BELVILE

Why, of an English elder brother's humour: educated in a nursery, with a maid to tend him till fifteen, and lies with his grandmother till he's of age; one that knows no pleasure beyond riding to the next fair, or going up to London with his right worshipful father in parliament time, wearing gay clothes, or making honourable love to his lady mother's laundry maid; gets drunk at a hunting match, and ten to one then gives some

264–5 *a broker . . . chains* All were associated with shrewd bargaining or persuasive argument.

267–8 *cried by the bellman* cried out for by the town crier.

271 *for Peru* as a slave in the mines of Peru.

273 *banged* beaten violently.

proofs of his prowess. – A pox upon him, he's our banker, and has all our cash about him; and if he fail, we are all broke.

FREDERICK

Oh, let him alone for that matter; he's of a damned stingy quality, that will secure our stock. I know not in what danger it were indeed if the jilt should pretend she's in love with him, for 'tis a kind believing coxcomb; otherwise, if he part with more than a piece of eight – geld him: for which offer he may chance to be beaten if she be a whore of the first rank.

BELVILE

Nay, the rogue will not be easily beaten; he's stout enough. Perhaps if they talk beyond his capacity he may chance to exercise his courage upon some of them, else I'm sure they'll find it as difficult to beat as to please him.

WILLMORE

'Tis a lucky devil to light upon so kind a wench!

FREDERICK

Thou hadst a great deal of talk with thy little gipsy; couldst thou do no good upon her? For mine was hard-hearted.

WILLMORE

Hang her, she was some damned honest person of quality, I'm sure; she was so very free and witty. If her face be but answerable to her wit and humour, I would be bound to constancy this month to gain her. In the meantime, have you made no kind acquaintance since you came to town? You do not use to be honest so long, gentlemen.

FREDERICK

Faith, love has kept us honest; we have been all fired with a beauty newly come to town, the famous Paduana Angellica Bianca.

WILLMORE

What, the mistress of the dead Spanish general?

283 *banker* the one elected to look after all their funds.
286 *stock* fund, i.e. sum of money set apart to provide for certain expenses.
287 *jilt* wench, prostitute.
289 *piece of eight* the old Spanish dollar.
298 *honest* chaste.
quality 1) high rank in society 2) wealth.
299 *free* 1) noble 2) unrestrained.
301–2 *made . . . acquaintance* met no willing women.
305 *Paduana* native of Padua.

BELVILE

Yes, she's now the only adored beauty of all the youth in Naples, who put on all their charms to appear lovely in her sight – their coaches, liveries, and themselves all gay as on a monarch's birthday to attract the eyes of this fair charmer, while she has the pleasure to behold all languish for her that see her.

FREDERICK

'Tis pretty to see with how much love the men regard her, and how much envy the women.

WILLMORE

What gallant has she?

BELVILE

None; she's exposed to sale, and four days in the week she's yours – for so much a month.

WILLMORE

The very thought of it quenches all manner of fire in me. Yet prithee, let's see her.

BELVILE

Let's first to dinner, and after that we'll pass the day as you please. But at night ye must all be at my devotion.

WILLMORE

I will not fail you.

[*Exeunt*]

310 *liveries* servants' uniforms.
315 *gallant* male champion.
316 *sale* ed. (sail Q1).
321 *at my devotion* dedicated to my sacred purpose, i.e. the rescue of Florinda.

ACT II, SCENE i

The long street

Enter BELVILE *and* FREDERICK *in masking habits, and* WILLMORE *in his own clothes, with a vizard in his hand*

WILLMORE
But why thus disguised and muzzled?

BELVILE
Because whatever extravagances we commit in these faces, our own may not be obliged to answer 'em.

WILLMORE
I should have changed my eternal buff, too; but no matter, my little gipsy would not have found me out then. For if she should change hers, it is impossible I should know her unless I should hear her prattle. A pox on't, I cannot get her out of my head. Pray Heaven, if ever I do see her again, she prove damnably ugly, that I may fortify myself against her tongue.

BELVILE
Have a care of love, for o' my conscience she was not of a quality to give thee any hopes.

WILLMORE
Pox on 'em, why do they draw a man in then? She has played with my heart so, that 'twill never lie still till I have met with some kind wench that will play the game out with me. Oh, for my arms full of soft, white, kind – woman! Such as I fancy Angellica.

BELVILE
This is her house, if you were but in stock to get admittance. They have not dined yet; I perceive the picture is not out.

Enter BLUNT

0 s.d. 2 *masking habits* See I.i.53 s.d. note.
s.d. 3 *vizard* face mask.
1 *muzzled* 1) masked 2) fitted with a restricting contraption over the mouth.
2 *faces* i.e. masks.
4 *buff* leather military coat.
17 *in stock* in funds, i.e. with financial means.
18 *the picture* i.e. of Angellica.

WILLMORE

I long to see the shadow of the fair substance; a man may gaze on that for nothing.

BLUNT

Colonel, thy hand. – And thine, Fred. I have been an ass, a deluded fool, a very coxcomb from my birth till this hour, and heartily repent my little faith.

BELVILE

What the devil's the matter with thee, Ned?

[BLUNT]

Oh, such a mistress.

FREDERICK

Such a girl!

WILLMORE

Ha! Where?

FREDERICK

Ay, where?

[BLUNT]

So fond, so amorous, so toying, and so fine! And all for sheer love, ye rogue! Oh, how she looked and kissed! And soothed my heart from my bosom! I cannot think I was awake, and yet methinks I see and feel her charms still. – Fred, try if she have not left the taste of her balmy kisses upon my lips –

Kisses him

BELVILE

Ha! Ha! Ha!

WILLMORE

Death, man, where is she?

21 *Colonel* ed. (Coll. Q1).

22 *coxcomb* See I.i.109 note.

25–8 lineation ed. (– Oh such a Mrs. *Fred.* such a Girl! / *Will.* Ha! where. *Fred.* Ay where! Q1).

25 s.p. *BLUNT* Q3 (om. Q1, Q2, C) The indented dash before 'Oh such' in Q1 suggests that a speech prefix is missing, and Blunt is the obvious candidate as Belvile has just addressed him.

26, 28 In Q1 Frederick's s.p. and speech run on with ll. 25 and 27 respectively.

29 s.p. *BLUNT* Q3, C (om. Q1, Q2). In Q1 the speech, which is characteristic of Blunt, is indented, as if a speech prefix is missing.

35 lineation Q3 (s.p. and speech run on with l. 34 Q1, Q2, C).

[BLUNT]

What a dog was I to stay in dull England so long! How have I laughed at the colonel when he sighed for love! But now the little archer has revenged him! And by this one dart I can guess at all his joys, which then I took for fancies, mere dreams and fables. Well, I'm resolved to sell all in Essex and plant here forever.

BELVILE

What a blessing 'tis, thou hast a mistress thou dar'st boast of; for I know thy humour is rather to have a proclaimed clap than a secret amour.

WILLMORE

Dost know her name?

BLUNT

Her name? No, 'sheartlikins. What care I for names? She's fair, young, brisk and kind, even to ravishment! And what a pox care I for knowing her by any other title?

WILLMORE

Didst give her anything?

BLUNT

Give her! Ha! Ha! Ha! Why, she's a person of quality. – That's a good one! Give her! 'Sheartlikins, dost think such creatures are to be bought? Or are we provided for such a purchase? Give her, quoth ye? Why, she presented me with this bracelet for the toy of a diamond I used to wear. No, gentlemen, Ned Blunt is not everybody. She expects me again tonight.

WILLMORE

Egad, that's well; we'll all go.

BLUNT

Not a soul! No, gentlemen, you are wits; I am a dull country rogue, I.

FREDERICK

Well, sir, for all your person of quality, I shall be very glad to understand your purse be secure; 'tis our whole estate at

36 s.p. *BLUNT* Q3, C (om. Q1, Q2) As at l. 25, an indented dash in Q1 suggests a missing speech prefix, and the reference to 'Essex' at l. 40 identifies Blunt as the speaker.
38 *little archer* Cupid.
40 *all in Essex* all his lands at home.
43 *proclaimed clap* apparent signs of gonorrhoea.
50 *quality* See I.ii.298 note.
56 *Egad* by God!.

present, which we are loath to hazard in one bottom. Come sir, unlade.

BLUNT

Take the necessary trifle useless now to me, that am beloved by such a gentlewoman. 'Sheartlikins, money! Here, take mine too.

FREDERICK

No, keep that to be cozened, that we may laugh.

WILLMORE

Cozened? Death! Would I could meet with one that would cozen me of all the love I could spare tonight.

FREDERICK

Pox, 'tis some common whore, upon my life.

BLUNT

A whore? Yes, with such clothes, such jewels, such a house, such furniture, and so attended! A whore!

BELVILE

Why yes, sir, they are whores, though they'll neither entertain you with drinking, swearing, or bawdry; are whores in all those gay clothes and right jewels; are whores with those great houses richly furnished with velvet beds, store of plate, handsome attendance, and fine coaches; are whores, and arrant ones.

WILLMORE

Pox on't, where do these fine whores live?

BELVILE

Where no rogues in office, ecliped constables, dare give 'em laws, nor the wine-inspired bullies of the town break their windows; yet they are whores though this Essex calf believe 'em persons of quality.

BLUNT

'Sheartlikins, y'are all fools. There are things about this Essex calf that shall take with the ladies, beyond all your wit and parts. This shape and size, gentlemen, are not to be despised; my waist, too, tolerably long, with other inviting signs that shall be nameless.

61 *bottom* ship, vessel.
62 *unlade* take the cargo out.
66 *cozened* cheated.
67 *cozen* beguile. 73 *right* genuine.
74 *plate* i.e. silver- or gold-plated ware.
75 *arrant* (errant Q1) unmitigated, thorough.
77 *ecliped* known as.
79 *Essex calf* foolish fellow.

WILLMORE

Egad, I believe he may have met with some person of quality that may be kind to him.

BELVILE

Dost thou perceive any such tempting things about him that should make a fine woman, and of quality, pick him out from all mankind to throw away her youth and beauty upon; nay, and her dear heart, too? No, no, Angellica has raised the price too high.

WILLMORE

May she languish for mankind till she die, and be damned for that one sin alone.

Enter two BRAVOS *and hang up a great picture of Angellica against the balcony, and two little ones at each side of the door* [*stating her terms*]

BELVILE

See there, the fair sign to the inn where a man may lodge that's fool enough to give her price.

WILLMORE *gazes on the picture*

BLUNT

'Sheartlikins, gentlemen, what's this?

BELVILE

A famous courtesan, that's to be sold.

BLUNT

How? To be sold? Nay, then I have nothing to say to her. Sold? What impudence is practised in this country? With what order and decency whoring's established here by virtue of the Inquisition! Come, let's be gone; I'm sure we're no chapmen for this commodity.

FREDERICK

Thou art none, I'm sure, unless thou couldst have her in thy bed at a price of a coach in the street.

91 *the price* i.e. of women's sexual favours.

93 *languish* waste away with desire for.

94 s.d. 1 BRAVOS See I.ii.118 note. *Angellica* ed. (Angellica's Q1).

98 *courtesan* euphemism for prostitute.

101–2 *the Inquisition* an ironic reference to a later form of the Roman Catholic medieval institution, authorised by Pope Sixtus IV in 1478 to combat heresy, witchcraft, and sorcery.

102 *chapmen* purchasers, customers.

WILLMORE

How wondrous fair she is. A thousand crowns a month? By Heaven, as many kingdoms were too little! A plague of this poverty, of which I ne'er complain but when it hinders my approach to beauty, which virtue ne'er could purchase.

Turns from the picture

BLUNT

What's this? – (*Reads*) 'A thousand crowns a month'! 'Sheartlikins, here's a sum! Sure 'tis a mistake. [*To one of the* BRAVOS] – Hark you, friend, does she take or give so much by the month?

FREDERICK

A thousand crowns! Why, 'tis a portion for the Infanta.

BLUNT

Hark ye, friends, won't she trust?

BRAVO

This is a trade, sir, that cannot live by credit.

Enter DON PEDRO *in masquerade, followed by* STEPHANO

BELVILE

See, here's more company; let's walk off a while.

Exeunt English [BELVILE, FREDERICK, WILLMORE, *and* BLUNT]

PEDRO *reads*

PEDRO

Fetch me a thousand crowns; I never wished to buy this beauty at an easier rate.

Passes off [*with* STEPHANO]

Enter ANGELLICA *and* MORETTA *in the balcony, and draw a silk curtain*

ANGELLICA [*To the* BRAVO]

Prithee, what said those fellows to thee?

BRAVO

Madam, the first were admirers of beauty only, but no purchasers; they were merry with your price and picture, laughed at the sum, and so passed off.

106 a *thousand crowns* A crown was 5 shillings (25p), so Angellica charged £250 a month – a large amount in the 1650s.

113 *portion . . . the Infanta* dowry . . . the daughter of the Spanish sovereign.

118 s.d. 3 *draw . . . curtain* presumably near the front of the balcony area (see l. 183 s.d.).

ANGELLICA

No matter, I'm not displeased with their rallying; their wonder feeds my vanity, and he that wishes but to buy gives me more pride than he that gives my price can make my pleasure.

BRAVO

Madam, the last I knew through all his disguises to be Don Pedro, nephew to the general, and who was with him in Pamplona.

ANGELLICA

Don Pedro? My old gallant's nephew! When his uncle died he left him a vast sum of money; it is he who was so in love with me at Padua, and who used to make the general so jealous.

MORETTA

Is this he that used to prance before our window, and take such care to show himself an amorous ass? If I am not mistaken, he is the likeliest man to give your price.

ANGELLICA

The man is brave and generous, but of an humour so uneasy and inconstant that the victory over his heart is as soon lost as won; a slave that can add little to the triumph of the conqueror. But inconstancy's the sin of all mankind, therefore I'm resolved that nothing but gold shall charm my heart.

MORETTA

I'm glad on't; 'tis only interest that women of our profession ought to consider, though I wonder what has kept you from that general disease of our sex so long; I mean that of being in love.

ANGELLICA

A kind but sullen star under which I had the happiness to be born. Yet I have had no time for love; the bravest and noblest of mankind have purchased my favours at so dear a rate, as if no coin but gold were current with our trade. – But here's Don Pedro again; fetch me my lute – for 'tis for him or Don Antonio, the viceroy's son, that I have spread my nets.

Enter at one door DON PEDRO [*and*] STEPHANO; DON ANTONIO *and* DIEGO [*his page*] *at the other door, with people following him in masquerade, anticly attired, some with music. They both go up to the picture*

123 *rallying* bantering, good-humoured ridicule.
127 *Pamplona* ed. (Pampalona Q1) See I.i.48 note.
128 *gallant* See I.ii.315 note.
148 s.d. 3 *anticly* bizarrely.

ANTONIO

A thousand crowns! Had not the painter flattered her, I should not think it dear.

PEDRO

Flattered her? By Heaven, he cannot. I have seen the original, nor is there one charm here more than adorns her face and eyes; all this soft and sweet, with a certain languishing air that no artist can represent.

ANTONIO

What I heard of her beauty before had fired my soul, but this confirmation of it has blown it to a flame.

PEDRO

Ha!

PAGE

Sir, I have known you throw away a thousand crowns on a worse face, and though y'are near your marriage, you may venture a little love here; Florinda will not miss it.

PEDRO (*Aside*)

Ha! Florinda! Sure 'tis Antonio.

ANTONIO

Florinda! Name not those distant joys; there's not one thought of her will check my passion here.

PEDRO (*Aside*)

Florinda scorned! (*A noise of a lute above*) And all my hopes defeated of the possession of Angellica! (ANTONIO *gazes up*) Her injuries, by Heaven, he shall not boast of!

Song to a lute above

SONG

[I]

When Damon first began to love
  He languished in a soft desire,
And knew not how the gods to move,
To lessen or increase his fire.
For Caelia in her charming eyes
Wore all love's sweets, and all his cruelties.

167 *Damon* Virgil's shepherd singer (eighth Eclogue): in poetry the name signified a rustic swain.

171 *Caelia* The name means 'heavenly'.

[II]

But as beneath a shade he lay,
Weaving of flowers for Caelia's hair,
She chanced to lead her flock that way,
And saw the am'rous shepherd there.
She gazed around upon the place,
And saw the grove, resembling night,
To all the joys of love invite,
Whilst guilty smiles and blushes dressed her face.
At this the bashful youth all transport grew,
And with kind force he taught the virgin how
To yield what all his sighs could never do.

ANGELLICA *throws open the curtains and bows to* ANTONIO, *who pulls off his vizard and bows and blows up kisses.* PEDRO, *unseen, looks in's face*

ANTONIO
By Heaven, she's charming fair!

PEDRO (*Aside*)
'Tis he, the false Antonio!

ANTONIO (*To the* BRAVO)
Friend, where must I pay my off'ring of love?
My thousand crowns I mean.

PEDRO
That off'ring I have designed to make,
And yours will come too late.

ANTONIO
Prithee begone; I shall grow angry else,
And then thou art not safe.

PEDRO
My anger may be fatal, sir, as yours,
And he that enters here may prove this truth.

ANTONIO
I know not who thou art, but I am sure thou'rt worth my killing, for aiming at Angellica.

They draw and fight

Enter WILLMORE *and* BLUNT, *who draw and part 'em*

BLUNT
'Sheartlikins, here's fine doings.

183 s.d. Q1, Q2 (follows l. 185 Q3, C).

WILLMORE

Tilting for the wench, I'm sure. Nay, gad, if that would win her I have as good a sword as the best of ye. – Put up, put up, and take another time and place, for this is designed for lovers only.

They all put up

PEDRO

We are prevented; dare you meet me tomorrow on the Molo?
For I've a title to a better quarrel,
That of Florinda, in whose credulous heart
Thou'st made an int'rest, and destroyed my hopes.

ANTONIO

Dare!
I'll meet thee there as early as the day.

PEDRO

We will come thus disguised, that whosoever chance to get the better, he may escape unknown.

ANTONIO

It shall be so.

Exeunt PEDRO *and* STEPHANO

Who should this rival be? Unless the English colonel, of whom I've often heard Don Pedro speak; it must be he, and time he were removed, who lays a claim to all my happiness.

WILLMORE *having gazed all this while on the picture, pulls down a little one*

WILLMORE

This posture's loose and negligent,
The sight on't would beget a warm desire
In souls whom impotence and age had chilled.
This must along with me.

BRAVO

What means this rudeness, sir? Restore the picture.

ANTONIO

Ha! Rudeness committed to the fair Angellica! – Restore the picture, sir.

197 *tilting* combating as in duelling.
198 *put up* put away, i.e. your swords.
200 *Molo* mall.
213 *beget* generate.
216 *Restore* replace.

WILLMORE
Indeed I will not, sir.

ANTONIO
By Heaven but you shall.

WILLMORE
Nay, do not show your sword; if you do, by this dear beauty – I will show mine too.

ANTONIO
What right can you pretend to't?

WILLMORE
That of possession which I will maintain. You, perhaps, have a 1000 crowns to give for the original.

ANTONIO
No matter, sir, you shall restore the picture.

ANGELLICA *and* MORETTA *[appear] above*

ANGELLICA
Oh Moretta! What's the matter?

ANTONIO *[To* WILLMORE*]*
Or leave your life behind.

WILLMORE
Death! You lie – I will do neither.

They fight. The Spaniards join with ANTONIO, BLUNT *laying on like mad*

ANGELLICA
Hold, I command you, if for me you fight.

They leave off and bow

WILLMORE
How heavenly fair she is! Ah plague of her price.

ANGELLICA
You, sir, in buff; you that appear a soldier, that first began this insolence –

WILLMORE
'Tis true, I did so, if you call it insolence for a man to preserve himself. I saw your charming picture and was wounded; quite

226 s.d. Q2 (s.d. follows l. 227 Q1, Q3, C).
229 s.d. ed. (after l. 230 Q1–3, C).
232 *buff* leather.

through my soul each pointed beauty ran; and wanting a thousand crowns to procure my remedy – I laid this little picture to my bosom – which if you cannot allow me, I'll resign.

ANGELLICA

No, you may keep the trifle.

ANTONIO

You shall first ask me leave, and this.

[They] fight again as before
Enter BELVILE *and* FREDERICK *who join with the English* [BLUNT *and* WILLMORE]

ANGELLICA

Hold! Will you ruin me! – Biskey – Sebastian! – Part 'em!

The Spaniards are beaten off

MORETTA

Oh madam, we're undone! A pox upon that rude fellow, he's set on to ruin us: we shall never see good days till all these fighting poor rogues are sent to the galleys.

Enter BELVILE, BLUNT, FREDERICK, *and* WILLMORE *with's shirt bloody*

BLUNT

'Sheartlikins, beat me at this sport, and I'll ne'er wear sword more.

BELVILE (*To* WILLMORE)

The devil's in thee for a mad fellow, thou art always one at an unlucky adventure – come let's begone whilst we're safe, and remember these are Spaniards, a sort of people that know how to revenge an affront.

FREDERICK

You bleed! I hope you are not wounded.

WILLMORE

Not much. A plague on your Dons; if they fight no better

236 *wanting* lacking.
238 *resign* relinquish.
241 s.d. *The Spaniards . . . off* Belvile, Blunt, Frederick, and Willmore exit, driving Antonio, Diego, and the bravos, Biskey and Sebastian, off-stage.
244 *the galleys* low flat-built vessels rowed by condemned criminals or slaves.
252 *Dons* Spaniards.

they'll ne'er recover Flanders. – What the devil was't to them that I took down the picture?

BLUNT

Took it! 'Sheartlikins we'll have the great one too; 'tis ours by conquest. – Prithee help me up and I'll pull it down –

ANGELLICA

Stay sir, and ere you affront me farther, let me know how you durst commit this outrage – to you I speak sir, for you appear a gentleman.

WILLMORE

To me, madam? – Gentlemen, your servant.

[*He is about to exit with* ANGELLICA;] BELVILE *stays him*

BELVILE

Is the devil in thee? Dost know the danger of ent'ring the house of an incensed courtesan?

WILLMORE

I thank you for your care – but there are other matters in hand, there are, though we have no great temptation. – Death! Let mc go!

FREDERICK

Yes, to your lodging if you will, but not in here. – Damn these gay harlots. – By this hand I'll have as sound and handsome a whore for a patacoon. – Death, man, she'll murder thee.

WILLMORE

Oh, fear me not! Shall I not venture where a beauty calls? A lovely charming beauty! For fear of danger! When, by Heaven, there's none so great as to long for her, whilst I want money to purchase her.

[FREDERICK]

Therefore 'tis loss of time unless you had the thousand crowns to pay.

WILLMORE

It may be she may give a favour; at least I shall have the pleasure of saluting her when I enter, and when I depart.

253 *they'll ne'er recover Flanders* In the late seventeenth century a large section of Flanders became French territory.

263–77 The dashes in Q1 could be meant to indicate that a physical struggle is taking place.

267 *patacoon* a Portuguese and Spanish silver coin worth about 24p.

272 s.p. *FREDERICK* Q3 (*PEDRO* Q1, Q2, C) Q3's emendation is necessary as Pedro left the stage at l. 208.

BELVILE

Pox, she'll as soon lie with thee as kiss thee, and sooner stab than do either. – You shall not go.

ANGELLICA

Fear not, sir; all I have to wound with is my eyes.

BLUNT [*To* BELVILE]

Let him go. 'Sheartlikins, I believe the gentlewoman means well.

BELVILE

Well, take thy fortune; we'll expect you in the next street. Farewell, fool. Farewell.

WILLMORE

Bye, colonel. *Goes in*

FREDERICK

The rogue's stark mad for a wench.

Exeunt

[ACT II,] SCENE [ii]

A fine chamber

Enter WILLMORE, ANGELLICA, *and* MORETTA

ANGELLICA

Insolent sir, how durst you pull down my picture?

WILLMORE

Rather, how durst you set it up to tempt poor am'rous mortals with so much excellence, which I find you have but too well consulted by the unmerciful price you set upon't. Is all this heaven of beauty shown to move despair in those that cannot buy? And can you think th'effects of that despair should be less extravagant than I have shown?

ANGELLICA

I sent for you to ask my pardon, sir, not to aggravate your crime. I thought I should have seen you at my feet imploring it.

278 *all . . . eyes* alluding to a Petrarchan conceit popular in sixteenth and seventeenth-century love poetry, in which the rejected lover claimed to have been slain by a cruel glance.

0 s.d. 1 See I.i.0 s.d. 1 note.

WILLMORE

You are deceived. I came to rail at you, and rail such truths, too, as shall let you see the vanity of that pride which taught you how to set such price on sin.
For such it is, whilst that which is love's due
Is meanly bartered for.

ANGELLICA

Ha! ha! ha! Alas, good captain, what pity 'tis your edifying doctrine will do no good upon me. – Moretta! Fetch the gentleman a glass, and let him survey himself. To see what charms he has (*Aside, in a soft tone*) – and guess my business.

MORETTA

He knows himself of old; I believe those breeches and he have been acquainted ever since he was beaten at Worcester.

ANGELLICA

Nay, do not abuse the poor creature –

MORETTA

Good weather-beaten corporal, will you march off? We have no need of your doctrine, though you have of our charity. But at present we have no scraps; we can afford no kindness for God's sake; in fine, sirrah, the price is too high i'th' mouth for you, therefore troop, I say.

WILLMORE [*To* MORETTA]

Here, good forewoman of the shop, serve me, and I'll be gone.

[*Offers her money*]

MORETTA

Keep it to pay your laundress, your linen stinks of the gun room – for here's no selling by retail.

WILLMORE

Thou hast sold plenty of thy stale ware at a cheap rate.

MORETTA

Ay, the more silly kind heart I; but this is an age wherein beauty is at higher rates. In fine, you know the price of this.

17 *glass* See I.ii.201 note.
19 *breeches* trousers which reach just below the knee.
20 *Worcester* On 3 September 1651 Cromwell finally defeated Charles II at Worcester and ended the Civil War.
25 *high i'th' mouth* To 'open one's mouth wide' meant to ask a high price.
26 *troop* be off.
27 *forewoman* manageress.

WILLMORE

I grant you 'tis here set down, a thousand crowns a month. Pray, how much may come to my share for a pistole? Bawd, take your black lead and sum it up, that I may have a pistole's worth of this vain gay thing, and I'll trouble you no more.

MORETTA

Pox on him, he'll fret me to death. – Abominable fellow, I tell thee, we only sell by the whole piece.

WILLMORE

'Tis very hard, the whole cargo or nothing. Faith, madam, my stock will not reach it; I cannot be your chapman. Yet I have countrymen in town, merchants of love like me; I'll see if they'll put in for a share. We cannot lose much by it, and what we have no use for, we'll sell upon the Friday's mart at 'Who gives more?' I am studying, madam, how to purchase you, though at present I am unprovided of money.

ANGELLICA [*Aside*]

Sure, this from any other man would anger me – nor shall he know the conquest he has made. – Poor angry man, how I despise this railing.

WILLMORE

Yes, I am poor – but I'm a gentleman,
And one that scorns this baseness which you practise.
Poor as I am, I would not sell myself.
No, not to gain your charming high-prized person.
Though I admire you strangely for your beauty,
Yet I condemn your mind.
And yet I would at any rate enjoy you;
At your own rate – but cannot. – See here
The only sum I can command on earth;
I know not where to eat when this is gone.
Yet such a slave I am to love and beauty
This last reserve I'll sacrifice to enjoy you.
Nay, do not frown; I know you're to be bought,
And would be bought by me. By me,

33 *here* i.e. on the picture he's holding.
34 *pistole* a Spanish gold coin worth between 82.5 and 90p.
35 *black-lead* pencil.
36 *thing* Q3 (things Q1, Q2, C).
40 *stock* funds. *chapman* purchaser.
43–4 *mart . . . more* auction.
55 *enjoy you* possess your body for my pleasure.

For a mean trifling sum if I could pay it down.
Which happy knowledge I will still repeat,
And lay it to my heart: it has a virtue in't,
And soon will cure those wounds your eyes have made.
And yet – there's something so divinely powerful there –
Nay, I will gaze – to let you see my strength.

Holds her, looks on her, and pauses and sighs

By Heaven, bright creature, I would not for the world
Thy fame were half so fair as is thy face.

Turns her away from him

ANGELLICA [*Aside*]
His words go through me to the very soul.
[*To him*] – If you have nothing else to say to me –

WILLMORE
Yes, you shall hear how infamous you are –
For which I do not hate thee –
But that secures my heart, and all the flames it feels
Are but so many lusts:
I know it by their sudden bold intrusion.
The fire's impatient and betrays; 'tis false –
For had it been the purer flame of love,
I should have pined and languished at your feet,
Ere found the impudence to have discovered it.
I now dare stand your scorn and your denial.

MORETTA [*Aside*]
Sure she's bewitched, that she can stand thus tamely and hear his saucy railing. – Sirrah, will you be gone?

ANGELLICA [*To* MORETTA]
How dare you take this liberty! Withdraw.

[MORETTA *withdraws, but remains on-stage*]

– Pray tell me, sir, are not you guilty of the same mercenary crime? When a lady is proposed to you for a wife, you never ask how fair, discreet, or virtuous she is, but 'What's her fortune?' – which, if but small, you cry, 'She will not do my business', and

66 *cure* Q1, Q3 (curse Q2, C).
wounds . . . eyes See II.i.278 note.
70 *fame* reputation.
83 *bewitched* Q2, Q3, C (bewitch Q1).

basely leave her, though she languish for you. Say, is not this as poor?

WILLMORE
It is a barbarous custom, which I will scorn to defend in our sex, and do despise in yours.

ANGELLICA
Thou'rt a brave fellow! Put up thy gold, and know,
That were thy fortune large as is thy soul,
Thou shouldst not buy my love
Couldst thou forget those mean effects of vanity
Which set me out to sale, and, as a lover,
Prize my yielding joys.
Canst thou believe they'll be entirely thine,
Without considering they were mercenary?

WILLMORE
I cannot tell; I must bethink me first – [*Aside*] – ha! Death, I'm going to believe her.

ANGELLICA
Prithee, confirm that faith – or if thou canst not – flatter me a little; 'twill please me from thy mouth.

WILLMORE (*Aside*)
Curse on thy charming tongue! Dost thou return
My feignèd contempt with so much subtlety?
[*To her*] – Thou'st found the easiest way into my heart,
Though I yet know that all thou say'st is false.

Turning from her in rage

ANGELLICA
By all that's good, 'tis real;
I never loved before, though oft a mistress.
Shall my first vows be slighted?

WILLMORE (*Aside*)
What can she mean?

ANGELLICA (*In an angry tone*)
I find you cannot credit me.

WILLMORE
I know you take me for an arrant ass,
An ass that may be soothed into belief,
And then be used at pleasure;

90 *though* Q2, Q3, C (thou Q1).
98 *which . . . lover,* ed. (which . . . joys. One line in Q1).

But, madam, I have been so often cheated
By perjured, soft, deluding hypocrites,
That I've no faith left for the cozening sex,
Especially for women of your trade.

ANGELLICA
The low esteem you have of me, perhaps
May bring my heart again:
For I have pride, that yet surmounts my love.

She turns with pride: he holds her

WILLMORE
Throw off this pride, this enemy to bliss,
And show the power of love: 'tis with those arms
I can be only vanquished, made a slave.

ANGELLICA
Is all my mighty expectation vanished?
No, I will not hear thee talk; thou hast a charm
In every word that draws my heart away.
And all the thousand trophies I designed
Thou hast undone. Why art thou soft?
Thy looks are bravely rough, and meant for war.
Could'st thou not storm on still?
I then, perhaps, had been as free as thou.

WILLMORE (*Aside*)
Death, how she throws her fire about my soul!
[*To her*] – Take heed, fair creature, how you raise my hopes,
Which once assumed pretend to all dominion.
There's not a joy thou hast in store,
I shall not then command.
For which I'll pay thee back my soul, my life!
Come, let's begin th'account this happy minute!

ANGELLICA
And will you pay me then the price I ask?

WILLMORE
Oh, why dost thou draw me from an awful worship,
By showing thou art no divinity.
Conceal the fiend, and show me all the angel!

124 s.d. *turns with pride:* ed. (turns: with pride Q1)
138 *pretend* ed. (pretends Q1).
144 *awful* full of awe, reverential.

Keep me but ignorant, and I'll be devout
And pay my vows forever at this shrine.

Kneels and kisses her hand

ANGELLICA
The pay I mean is but thy love for mine.
Can you give that?

WILLMORE
Entirely. Come, let's withdraw where I'll renew my vows – and breathe 'em with such ardour thou shalt not doubt my zeal.

ANGELLICA
Thou hast a power too strong to be resisted.

Exeunt WILLMORE *and* ANGELLICA

MORETTA
Now my curse go with you! Is all our project fallen to this? To love the only enemy to our trade? Nay, to love such a shameroon, a very beggar; nay, a pirate beggar, whose business is to rifle and be gone; a no-purchase, no-pay tatterdemalion, and English picaroon – a rogue that fights for daily drink, and takes a pride in being loyally lousy? Oh, I could curse now, if I durst. This is the fate of most whores.

Trophies, which from believing fops we win,
Are spoils to those who cozen us again.

[*Exit*]

155–6 *shameroon* shameful person.
157 *tatterdemalion* ragamuffin, beggar.
158 *picaroon* pirate, brigand watching out to seize a prize.

ACT III, SCENE i

A street

Enter FLORINDA, VALERIA, HELLENA, *in antic different dresses from what they were in before,* CALLIS *attending*

FLORINDA

I wonder what should make my brother in so ill a humour? I hope he has not found out our ramble this morning.

HELLENA

No, if he had, we should have heard on't at both ears, and have been mewed up this afternoon; which I would not for the world should have happened. Hey, ho, I'm as sad as a lover's lute.

VALERIA

Well, methinks we have learnt this trade of gipsies as readily as if we had been bred upon the road to Loretta: and yet I did so fumble, when I told the stranger his fortune, that I was afraid I should have told my own and yours by mistake. But, methinks Hellena has been very serious ever since.

FLORINDA

I would give my garters she were in love, to be revenged upon her for abusing me. – How is't, Hellena?

HELLENA

Ah, would I had never seen my mad monsieur – and yet for all your laughing, I am not in love – and yet this small acquaintance o' my conscience will never out of my head.

VALERIA

Ha, ha, ha! I laugh to think how thou art fitted with a lover, a fellow that I warrant loves every new face he sees.

HELLENA

Hum, he has not kept his word with me here, and may be taken up – that thought is not very pleasant to me. What the deuce should this be now that I feel?

0 s.d. 2 *antic* bizarre.
2 *ramble* See I.i.179 note.
4 *mewed* shut.
5 *I'm as* Q1–3 (I'm, C).
18–19 *taken up* i.e. occupied with a new woman.
19 *deuce* devil.

VALERIA

What is't like?

HELLENA

Nay, the Lord knows – but if I should be hanged I cannot choose but be angry and afraid when I think that mad fellow should be in love with anybody but me: what to think of myself, I know not. Would I could meet with some true damned gipsy that I might know my fortune.

VALERIA

Know it! Why there's nothing so easy. Thou wilt love this wandering inconstant till thou find'st thyself hanged about his neck, and then be as mad to get free again.

FLORINDA

Yes, Valeria, we shall see her bestride his baggage horse and follow him to the campaign.

HELLENA

So, so, now you are provided for, there's no care taken of poor me: but since you have set my heart a-wishing, I am resolved to know for what. I will not die of the pip, so I will not.

FLORINDA

Art thou mad to talk so? Who will like thee well enough to have thee, that hears what a mad wench thou art?

HELLENA

Like me! I don't intend every he that likes me shall have me, but he that I like. I should have stayed in the nunnery still if I had liked my Lady Abbess as well as she liked me. No, I came thence not, as my wise brother imagines, to take an eternal farewell of the world, but to love and to be beloved; and I will be beloved, or I'll get one of your men, so I will.

VALERIA

Am I put into the number of lovers?

HELLENA

You? Why coz, I know thou'rt too good-natured to leave us in any design: thou wouldst venture a cast though thou camest off a loser, especially with such a gamester. I observe your man, and

34 *pip* a humorous general term for an ailment (in this case, being loveless).

44 *coz* cousin (used fondly of relatives and close friends).

45 *design* scheme.
wouldst ed. (wou't, Q1, Q2; would Q3; won't C).
venture a cast risk a throw of the dice.
camest ed. (comest Q1).

your willing ear incline that way; and if you are not a lover, 'tis an art soon learnt (*Sighs*) – that I find.

FLORINDA

I wonder how you learnt to love so easily. I had a thousand charms to meet my eyes and ears ere I could yield, and 'twas the knowledge of Belvile's merit, not the surprising person, took my soul. Thou art too rash, to give a heart at first sight.

HELLENA

Hang your considering lover! I never thought beyond the fancy that 'twas a very pretty, idle, silly kind of pleasure to pass one's time with: to write little, soft, nonsensical *billets*, and with great difficulty and danger, receive answers in which I shall have my beauty praised, my wit admired – though little or none – and have the vanity and power to know I am desirable. Then I have the more inclination that way because I am to be a nun, and so shall not be suspected to have any such earthly thoughts about me, but when I walk thus – and sigh thus – they'll think my mind's upon my monastery, and cry, 'How happy 'tis she's so resolved'. But not a word of man.

FLORINDA

What a mad creature's this?

HELLENA

I'll warrant, if my brother hears either of you sigh, he cries gravely: 'I fear you have the indiscretion to be in love, but take heed of the honour of our house and your own unspotted fame', and so he conjures on till he has laid the soft winged god in your hearts, or broke the bird's nest. – But see, here comes your lover, but where's my inconstant? Let's step aside and we may learn something.

[*They*] *go aside*

Enter BELVILE, FREDERICK, *and* BLUNT

BELVILE

What means this! The picture's taken in.

55 *soft . . . billets* billets-doux, love letters.
63 *But . . . man.* separate line in Q1.
a Q2, Q3, C (om. Q1).
68 *soft winged god* Cupid.
68–9 *laid . . . nest* i.e. until his behaviour has strengthened your resolution to love or has destroyed it.

BLUNT

It may be the wench is good-natured and will be kind gratis. Your friend's a proper handsome fellow.

BELVILE

I rather think she has cut his throat and is fled: I am mad he should throw himself into dangers. Pox on't, I shall want him, too, at night. Let's knock and ask for him.

HELLENA

My heart goes a-pit, a-pat, for fear 'tis my man they talk of.

[BELVILE *and* BLUNT] *knock;* MORETTA [*appears*] *above*

MORETTA

What would you have?

BELVILE

Tell the stranger that entered here about two hours ago that his friends stay here for him.

MORETTA

A curse upon him for Moretta! Would he were at the devil – but he's coming to you.

[*Enter* WILLMORE]

HELLENA

I, I, 'tis he! Oh, how this vexes me.

BELVILE

And how, and how dear lad, has fortune smiled? Are we to break her windows, or raise up altars to her, ha?

WILLMORE

Does not my fortune sit triumphant on my brow? Dost not see the little wanton god there, all gay and smiling? Have I not an air about my face and eyes that distinguish me from the crowd of common lovers? By Heaven, Cupid's quiver has not half so many darts as her eyes! Oh, such a *bona roba*! To sleep in her arms is lying in *fresco*, all perfumed air about me.

HELLENA (*Aside*)

Here's fine encouragement for me to fool on.

73 *be kind gratis* give her sexual favours free of charge.

74 *proper* See I.i.36 note.

76–7 *want . . . night* i.e. lack his help tonight (in Florinda's rescue).

77 *too, at night* ed. (too at Night Q1, Q3; tonight Q2, C).

81 *stay* wait.

91 *bona roba* It. *buona* (good) *roba* (robe, dress, stuff): 'a showy wanton' (*OED*).

92 *in fresco* in the fresh air.

WILLMORE

Hark'ee, where didst thou purchase that rich Canary we drank today? Tell me, that I may adore the spigot and sacrifice to the butt! The juice was divine – into which I must dip my rosary, and then bless all things that I would have bold or fortunate!

BELVILE

Well sir, let's go take a bottle and hear the story of your success.

FREDERICK

Would not French wine do better?

WILLMORE

Damn the hungry balderdash! Cheerful sack has a generous virtue in't inspiring a successful confidence, gives eloquence to the tongue and vigour to the soul, and has, in a few hours, completed all my hopes and wishes! There's nothing left to raise a new desire in me. Come, let's be gay and wanton – and gentlemen, study; study what you want, for here are friends that will supply, gentlemen. [*He jingles coins*] Hark, what a charming sound they make! 'Tis he and she gold whil'st here, and shall beget new pleasures every moment.

BLUNT

But hark'ee, sir, you are not married are you?

WILLMORE

All the honey of matrimony, but none of the sting, friend.

BLUNT

'Sheartlikins, thou'rt a fortunate rogue!

WILLMORE

I am so, sir; let these [*Chinking the coins*] inform you! Ha, how sweetly they chime! Pox of poverty: it makes a man a slave, makes wit and honour sneak. My soul grew lean and rusty for want of credit.

BLUNT

'Sheartlikins, this I like well; it looks like my lucky bargain! Oh, how I long for the approach of my squire that is to conduct me to her house again. Why, here's two provided for!

94 *Canary* sweet wine from the Canary Islands

95 *spigot* wooden peg of a cask. 96 *butt* cask.

99 *French* ed. (Frenoh Q1).

100 *hungry balderdash* deficient jumbled mixture of liquors.
sack white wine from Spain and the Canaries.

101 *confidence, gives* confidence which gives.

107 *he and she* C2 (he and the Q1, Q2, C; the he and the she Q3).
whil'st i.e. whilest, passes time idly.

FREDERICK
By this light, y'are happy men.

BLUNT
Fortune is pleased to smile on us, gentlemen – to smile on us.

Enter SANCHO *and pulls down* BLUNT *by the sleeve. They go aside*

SANCHO
Sir, my lady expects you. She has removed all that might oppose your will and pleasure – and is impatient till you come.

BLUNT
Sir, I'll attend you. – Oh, the happiest rogue! I'll take no leave, lest they either dog me or stay me.

Exit with SANCHO

BELVILE
But then the little gipsy is forgot?

WILLMORE
A mischief on thee for putting her into my thoughts. I had quite forgot her else, and this night's debauch had drunk her quite down.

HELLENA
Had it so, good captain!

Claps him on the back

WILLMORE (*Aside*)
Ha! I hope she did not hear me.

HELLENA
What, afraid of such a champion?

WILLMORE
Oh, you're a fine lady of your word, are you not? To make a man languish a whole day –

HELLENA
In tedious search of me.

WILLMORE
Egad, child, thou'rt in the right. Hadst thou seen what a melancholy dog I have been ever since I was a lover, how I have walked the streets like a Capuchin, with my hands in my sleeves – faith, sweetheart, thou wouldst pity me.

124 *dog* follow.
137 *Capuchin* a hooded friar of the order of St Francis's austere new rule, 1528.

HELLENA (*Aside*)

Now, if I should be hanged I can't be angry with him, he dissembles so heartily. – Alas, good captain, what pains you have taken; now were I ungrateful not to reward so true a servant.

WILLMORE

Poor soul, that's kindly said! I see thou bearest a conscience. Come then, for a beginning, show me thy dear face.

HELLENA

I'm afraid, my small acquaintance, you have been staying that swinging stomach you boasted of this morning. I then remember my little collation would have gone down with you without the sauce of a handsome face. Is your stomach so queasy now?

WILLMORE

Faith, long fasting, child, spoils a man's appetite. Yet, if you durst treat, I could so lay about me still –

HELLENA

And would you fall to before a priest says grace?

WILLMORE

Oh, fie, fie, what an old, out-of-fashioned thing hast thou named? Thou couldst not dash me more out of countenance shouldst thou show me an ugly face.

Whilst he is seemingly courting HELLENA, *enter* ANGELLICA, MORETTA, BISKEY, *and* SEBASTIAN, *all in masquerade.* ANGELLICA *sees* WILLMORE *and stares*

ANGELLICA

Heavens, 'tis he! And passionately fond to see another woman!

MORETTA

What could you less expect from such a swaggerer?

ANGELLICA

Expect? As much as I paid him – a heart entire
Which I had pride enough to think, when'er I gave,
It would have raised the man above the vulgar,
Made him all soul, and that all soft and constant!

142 *bearest* C (barest Q1–3).

144 *small acquaintance* i.e. person I have known only slightly.
staying sustaining, strengthening.

146 *collation* light meal that needs little preparation.

147 *queasy* 1) easily upset 2) uncertain.

150 *fall to* i.e. begin eating.

153 s.d. 3 *stares* Q1–3 (starts C).

154 *'tis* Q3 ('ts Q1; it's Q2; is't C).

HELLENA

You see, captain, how willing I am to be friends with you, till time and ill luck make us lovers, and ask you the question first, rather than put your modesty to the blush by asking me. For, alas! I know you captains are such strict men, and such severe observers of your vows to chastity, that 'twill be hard to prevail with your tender conscience to marry a young willing maid!

WILLMORE

Do not abuse me, for fear I should take thee at thy word and marry thee indeed, which I'm sure will be revenge sufficient.

HELLENA

O' my conscience, that will be our destiny because we are both of one humour. I am as inconstant as you, for I have considered, captain, that a handsome woman has a great deal to do whilst her face is good, for then is our harvest-time to gather friends; and should I, in these days of my youth, catch a fit of foolish constancy, I were undone: 'tis loitering by daylight in our great journey. Therefore I declare, I'll allow but one year for love, one year for indifference, and one year for hate, and then – go hang yourself – for I protest myself the gay, the kind, and the inconstant. The devil's in't if this won't please you.

WILLMORE

Oh, most damnably. I have a heart with a hole quite through it, too; no prison, mine, to keep a mistress in.

ANGELLICA (*Aside*)

Perjured man! How I believe thee now.

HELLENA

Well, I see our business as well as humours are alike: yours to cozen as many maids as will trust you, and I as many men as have faith. See if I have not as desperate a lying look as you can have for the heart of you. (*Pulls off her vizard: he starts*) How do you like it, captain?

WILLMORE

Like it! By Heaven, I never saw so much beauty! Oh, the charms of those sprightly black eyes! That strangely fair face, full of smiles and dimples! Those soft, round, melting cherry lips and small, even, white teeth! Not to be expressed, but silently adored! [*She replaces her mask*] Oh, one look more, and strike me dumb or I shall repeat nothing else till I'm mad!

He seems to court her to pull off her vizard: she refuses

ANGELLICA

I can endure no more. Nor is it fit to interrupt him, for if I do, my jealousy has so destroyed my reason, I shall undo him. Therefore I'll retire – and you, Sebastian (*To one of her* BRAVOS), follow that woman and learn who 'tis; while you (*To the other* BRAVO) tell the fugitive I would speak to him instantly.

Exit

This while FLORINDA [*in disguise*] *is talking to* BELVILE, *who stands sullenly,* FREDERICK *courting* VALERIA

VALERIA

Prithee, dear stranger, be not so sullen, for though you have lost your love, you see my friend frankly offers you hers to play with in the meantime.

BELVILE

Faith, madam, I am sorry I can't play at her game.

FREDERICK

Pray leave your intercession and mind your own affair. They'll better agree apart; he's a modest sigher in company, but alone, no woman 'scapes him.

FLORINDA [*Aside*]

Sure, he does but rally – yet if it should be true? I'll tempt him farther. – Believe me, noble stranger, I'm no common mistress. And for a little proof on't – wear this jewel. Nay, take it, sir, 'tis right, and bills of exchange may sometimes miscarry.

BELVILE

Madam, why am I chosen out of all mankind to be the object of your bounty?

VALERIA

There's another civil question asked.

FREDERICK

Pox of's modesty; it spoils his own markets and hinders mine.

FLORINDA

Sir, from my window I have often seen you, and women of my quality have so few opportunities for love that we ought to lose

204 *rally* banter, make fun (of Belvile).
206 *jewel* her portrait in miniature, in a locket or on a chain. She may be attempting to hang this round his neck.
207 *bills of exchange* written orders to pay a given sum on a specified date.
208 *chosen* ed. (chose Q1).

none.

FREDERICK

Ay, this is something! Here's a woman! When shall I be blessed with so much kindness from your fair mouth? (*Aside to* BELVILE) – Take the jewel, fool.

BELVILE

You tempt me strangely, madam, every way.

FLORINDA (*Aside*)

So, if I find him false, my whole repose is gone.

BELVILE

And but for a vow I've made to a very fair lady, this goodness had subdued me.

FREDERICK [*Aside to* BELVILE]

Pox on't, be kind; in pity to me, be kind, for I am to thrive here but as you treat her friend.

HELLENA [*To* WILLMORE]

Tell me what you did in yonder house, and I'll unmask.

WILLMORE

Yonder house? Oh – I went to – a – to – why, there's a friend of mine lives there.

HELLENA

What, a she or a he friend?

WILLMOR

A man upon honour! A man. – A she friend? No, no, madam, you have done my business, I thank you.

HELLENA

And was't your man friend that had more darts in's eyes than Cupid carries in's whole budget of arrows?

WILLMORE

So –

HELLENA

'Ah, such a *bona roba*! To be in her arms is lying in *fresco*, all perfumed air about me.' – Was this your man friend too?

WILLMORE

So –

HELLENA

That gave you the he and the she gold that begets young pleasures?

220 *fair* some copies Q1 (B.L.644.g.12), Q3 (om. some copies Q1, Q2, C).
231 *budget* quiver.
236 *the . . . gold* See l. 107.

WILLMORE
Well, well, madam, then you see there are ladies in the world that will not be cruel. There are, madam, there are –

HELLENA
And there be men, too, as fine, wild, inconstant fellows as yourself. There be, captain, there be, if you go to that now. Therefore I'm resolved –

WILLMORE
Oh!

HELLENA
To see your face no more –

WILLMORE
Oh!

HELLENA
Till tomorrow.

WILLMORE
Egad, you frighted me.

HELLENA
Nor then neither, unless you'll swear never to see that lady more.

WILLMORE
See her! Why, never to think of womankind again.

HELLENA
Kneel – and swear.

[WILLMORE] *kneels; she gives him her hand*

WILLMORE
I do – never to think, to see, to love, nor lie – with any but thyself.

HELLENA
Kiss the book.

WILLMORE
Oh, most religiously.

Kisses her hand

HELLENA
Now, what a wicked creature am I, to damn a proper fellow.

CALLIS (*To* FLORINDA)
Madam, I'll stay no longer; 'tis e'en dark.

251 *I do – never . . . think, . . . see, . . . love,* ed. (I do never . . . think – to see – to love – nor Lye Q1).

253 *kiss . . . book* as if swearing on the Bible, here replaced by her hand.

FLORINDA [*To* BELVILE]

However, sir, I'll leave this with you – that when I'm gone, you may repent the opportunity you have lost by your modesty.

Gives him the jewel, which is her picture, and exits. He gazes after her

WILLMORE [*To* HELLENA]

'Twill be an age till tomorrow – and till then, I will most impatiently expect you. Adieu, my dear, pretty angel.

Exeunt all the women

BELVILE

Ha! Florinda's picture! 'Twas she herself – what a dull dog was I! I would have given the world for one minute's discourse with her.

FREDERICK

This comes of your modesty! Ah, pox o' your vow; 'twas ten to one but we had lost the jewel by't.

BELVILE

Willmore! The blessed'st opportunity lost! Florinda! Friends! Florinda!

WILLMORE

Ah, rogue! Such black eyes! Such a face! Such a mouth! Such teeth – and so much wit!

BELVILE

All, all, and a thousand charms besides.

WILLMORE

Why, dost thou know her?

BELVILE

Know her! Ay, ay, and a pox take me with all my heart for being modest.

WILLMORE

But hark'ee, friend of mine, are you my rival? And have I been only beating the bush all this while?

BELVILE

I understand thee not. I'm mad – see here –

Shows the picture [*of* FLORINDA]

WILLMORE

Ha! Whose picture's this? 'Tis a fine wench!

275 *beating the bush* i.e. so that the game (Hellena) will be roused and driven towards Belvile rather than himself.

FREDERICK
The colonel's mistress, sir.

WILLMORE
Oh, oh, here – (*Gives the picture back*). I thought 't had been another prize. Come, come, a bottle will set thee right again.

BELVILE
I am content to try, and by that time 'twill be late enough for our design.

WILLMORE
Agreed.
Love does all day the soul's great empire keep,
But wine at night lulls the soft god asleep.

Exeunt

[ACT III,] SCENE ii

Lucetta's house

Enter BLUNT *and* LUCETTA *with a light*

LUCETTA
Now we are safe and free; no fears of the coming home of my old jealous husband, which made me a little thoughtful when you came in first – but now love is all the business of my soul.

BLUNT (*Aside*)
I am transported! Pox on't that I had but some fine things to say to her, such as lovers use – I was a fool not to learn of Fred a little by heart before I came. Something I must say. [*To her*] – 'Sheartlikins, sweet soul! I am not used to compliment, but I'm an honest gentleman, and thy humble servant.

LUCETTA
I have nothing to pay for so great a favour, but such a love as cannot but be great, since at first sight of that sweet face and shape it made me your absolute captive.

BLUNT [*Aside*]
Kind heart! How prettily she talks! Egad, I'll show her husband

284–5 Perhaps the final lines are sung off-stage.

a Spanish trick; send him out of the world and marry her: she's damnably in love with me, and will ne'er mind settlements, and so there's that saved.

LUCETTA

Well, sir, I'll go and undress me, and be with you instantly.

BLUNT

Make haste then, for 'adsheartlikins, dear soul, thou canst not guess at the pain of a longing lover when his joys are drawn within the compass of a few minutes.

LUCETTA

You speak my sense, and I'll make haste to prove it. *Exit*

BLUNT

'Tis a rare girl, and this one night's enjoyment with her will be worth all the days I ever passed in Essex! Would she would go with me into England; though, to say truth, there's plenty of whores already. But a pox on 'em, they are such mercenary, prodigal whores, that they want such a one as this, that's free and generous, to give 'em good examples. – Why, what a house she has; how rich and fine!

Enter SANCHO

SANCHO

Sir, my lady has sent me to conduct you to her chamber.

BLUNT

Sir, I shall be proud to follow. – Here's one of her servants, too! 'Sheartlikins, by this garb and gravity he might be a Justice of Peace in Essex, and is but a pimp here.

Exeunt [BLUNT *and* SANCHO]

13 *Spanish* i.e. synonymous with 'treacherous' to the English at this time.
14 *settlements* the settling of property upon a person, e.g. before marriage.
17 *'adsheartlikins* By God's little heart (see I.ii.13 note).
18 *drawn* drawn out.
20 *prove* Q1, Q3 (provide Q2 and C, where the speech is an aside).
30–1 *Justice of Peace* an important official in the seventeenth century.

[ACT III, SCENE iii]

The scene changes to a chamber with an alcove bed in't, a table, etc., LUCETTA *in bed. Enter* SANCHO *and* BLUNT, *who takes the candle of* SANCHO *at the door*

SANCHO
Sir, my commission reaches no farther. [*Exit*]

BLUNT
Sir, I'll excuse your compliment. [*He locks the door after* SANCHO] – What, in bed, my sweet mistress?

LUCETTA
You see, I still out-do you in kindness.

BLUNT
And thou shalt see what haste I'll make to quit scores – oh, the luckiest rogue!

He undresses himself

LUCETTA
Should you be false or cruel now!

BLUNT
False! 'Sheartlikins, what dost thou take me for? A Jew? An insensible heathen? A pox of thy old jealous husband; an he were dead – egad, sweet soul – it should be none of my fault if I did not marry thee.

LUCETTA
It never should be mine.

BLUNT
Good soul! I'm the fortunatest dog!

LUCETTA
Are you not undressed yet?

BLUNT
As much as my impatience will permit.

Goes towards the bed in his shirt [and] drawers

LUCETTA
Hold, sir, put out the light; it may betray us else.

BLUNT
Anything! I need no other light but that of thine eyes! – 'Sheartlikins, there, I think I had it.

[He] puts out the candle; the bed descends; he gropes about to find it

Why, why – where am I got? What, not yet? – Where are you, sweetest? – Ah, the rogue's silent now. A pretty love-trick, this – how she'll laugh at me anon! You need not, my dear rogue! You need not! I'm all on fire already. – Come, come, now call me in pity. – Sure, I'm enchanted! I have been round the chamber and can find neither woman, nor bed. I locked the door; I'm sure she cannot go that way – or if she could, the bed could not. – Enough, enough, my pretty wanton; do not carry the jest too far. (*Lights on a trap and is let down*) – Ha, betrayed! Dogs! Rogues! Pimps! – Help! Help!

Enter LUCETTA, PHILIPPO, *and* SANCHO *with a light*

PHILIPPO
Ha, ha, ha! He's dispatched finely.

LUCETTA
Now, sir, had I been coy, we had missed of this booty.

PHILIPPO
Nay, when I saw 'twas a substantial fool, I was mollified; but when you dote upon a serenading coxcomb, upon a face, fine clothes, and a lute, it makes me rage.

LUCETTA
You know I was never guilty of that folly, my dear Philippo, but with yourself – but come, let's see what we have got by this.

PHILIPPO
A rich coat – sword and hat! – These breeches, too, are well-lined. – See here, a gold watch! – A purse, ha! Gold! At least two hundred pistoles! – A bunch of diamond rings, and one with the family arms! – A gold box, with a medal of his king, and his lady mother's picture! These were sacred relics, believe me! – See, the waistband of his breeches have a mine of gold – old Queen Bess's! We have a quarrel to her ever since eighty-eight,

18 s.d. 1 *bed descends* i.e. beneath the stage, through a trapdoor operated by machinery under the stage.
27 s.d. *Lights . . . down* Blunt stands on a trapdoor which, when activated, drops him into the space below the stage (perhaps the concealed bed breaks his fall if the same trap is used).
29 *dispatched* ed. (dispatch Q1).
39 *his king* Charles II.
42 *eighty-eight* 1588, the year of the Spanish Armada's defeat.

and may, therefore, justify the theft: the Inquisition might have committed it.

LUCETTA

– See, a bracelet of bowed gold! These, his sisters tied about his arm at parting. But well – for all this, I fear his being a stranger may make a noise and hinder our trade with them hereafter.

PHILIPPO

That's our security; he is not only a stranger to us, but to the country, too. The common sewer into which he is descended, thou knowest, conducts him into another street, which this light will hinder him from ever finding again. He knows neither your name, nor that of the street where your house is; nay, nor the way to his own lodgings.

LUCETTA

And art not thou an unmerciful rogue? Not to afford him one night for all this! I should not have been such a Jew.

PHILIPPO

Blame me not, Lucetta, to keep as much of thee as I can to myself. Come, that thought makes me wanton! Let's to bed! – Sancho, lock up these.

This is the fleece which fools do bear,
Designed for witty men to shear.

Exeunt [LUCETTA, PHILIPPO, *and* SANCHO]

[ACT III, SCENE iv]

The scene changes, and discovers BLUNT *creeping out of a common sewer, his face, etc. all dirty*

BLUNT (*Climbing up*)

Oh Lord! I am got out at last and, which is a miracle, without a clue. And now to damning and cursing! But if that would ease me, where shall I begin? With my fortune, myself, or the quean

45 *bowed* curved.
49 *sewer* ed. (shoar Q1).

0 s.d. 1 *discovers* reveals.
s.d. 2 *sewer* ed. (shoar Q1).
3 *quean* hussy (queen C).

that cozened me? What a dog was I to believe in Woman? Oh, coxcomb! Ignorant, conceited coxcomb! To fancy she could be enamoured with my person! At first sight, enamoured! Oh, I'm a cursed puppy! 'Tis plain, 'Fool' was writ upon my forehead! She perceived it – saw the Essex calf there. For what allurements could there be in this countenance, which I can endure because I'm acquainted with it? Oh, dull, silly dog! To be thus soothed into a cozening! Had I been drunk, I might fondly have credited the young quean! But as I was in my right wits, to be thus cheated confirms it I am a dull, believing, English country fop. – But my comrades! Death and the devil, there's the worst of all! Then a ballad will be sung tomorrow on the Prado, to a lousy tune of the Enchanted Squire and the Annihilated Damsel. – But Fred, that rogue, and the colonel will abuse me beyond all Christian patience! Had she left me my clothes, I have a bill of exchange at home would've saved my credit – but now all hope is taken from me. Well, I'll home – if I can find the way – with this consolation, that I am not the first kind, believing coxcomb, but there are, gallants, many such good natures amongst ye.

And though you've better arts to hide your follies,
'Adsheartlikins, y'are all as arrant cullies. [*Exit*]

[ACT III,] SCENE [v]

The garden in the night

Enter FLORINDA *in an undress, with a key and a little box*

FLORINDA

Well, thus far I'm in my way to happiness. I have got myself free from Callis; my brother, too, I find by yonder light, is got into

4 *cozened* See II.i.66 note. *Woman* Q1-3 (Women C).
5 *coxcomb* See I.i.109 note.
8 *Essex calf* See II.i.79 note.
13 *confirms it I* Q1, Q3 (confirms I Q2, C).
15 *Prado* a fashionable promenade, i.e. a popular public place.
24 *cullies* dupes, simpletons.
s.d. Q3 (om. Q1, Q2, C).

0 s.d. 2 *an undress* partial or incomplete clothing.

his cabinet and thinks not of me. I have, by good fortune, got the key of the garden back-door. I'll open it to prevent Belvile's knocking: a little noise will now alarm my brother. Now am I as fearful as a young thief. (*Unlocks the door*) – Hark! What noise is that? Oh, 'twas the wind that played amongst the boughs. Belvile stays long, methinks – it's time. Stay, for fear of a surprise, I'll hide these jewels in yonder jasmine.

She goes to lay down the box

Enter WILLMORE *drunk*

WILLMORE

What the devil is become of these fellows, Belvile and Frederick? They promised to stay at the next corner for me, but who the devil knows the corner of a full moon? Now, whereabouts am I? – Ha, what have we here? A garden! A very convenient place to sleep in. – Ha, what has God sent us here? A female – by this light, a woman! I'm a dog if it be not a very wench!

FLORINDA

He's come! – Ha, who's there?

WILLMORE

Sweet soul, let me salute thy shoe-string!

FLORINDA [*Aside*]

'Tis not my Belvile. Good Heavens! I know him not. – Who are you, and from whence come you?

WILLMORE

Prithee, prithee, child – not so many hard questions. Let it suffice I am here, child. – Come, come kiss me.

FLORINDA

Good gods! What luck is mine?

WILLMORE

Only good luck, child, parlous good luck. Come hither. – 'Tis a delicate, shining wench! By this hand, she's perfumed, and smells like any nosegay. – Prithee, dear soul, let's not play the fool and lose time, precious time; for as Gad shall save me, I'm as honest a fellow as breathes, though I'm a little disguised at

3 *cabinet* a small private apartment.
11 *stay* See I.i.188 note.
24 *parlous* extraordinary.
28 *disguised* drunk.

present. – Come, I say. – Why, thou may'st be free with me; I'll be very secret. I'll not boast who 'twas obliged me, not I – for hang me if I know thy name.

FLORINDA

Heavens! What a filthy beast is this?

WILLMORE

I am so, and thou ought'st the sooner to lie with me for that reason. For look you, child, there will be no sin in't because 'twas neither designed, nor premeditated. 'Tis pure accident on both sides – that's a certain thing now. Indeed, should I make love to you, and you vow fidelity – and swear and lie till you believed and yielded – that were to make it wilful fornication, the crying sin of the nation. Thou art, therefore – as thou art a good Christian – obliged in conscience to deny me nothing. Now – come, be kind without any more idle prating.

FLORINDA

Oh, I am ruined! – Wicked man, unhand me.

WILLMORE

Wicked! Egad, child, a judge, were he young and vigorous, and saw those eyes of thine, would know 'twas they gave the first blow – the first provocation. Come, prithee, let's lose no time, I say. This is a fine, convenient place.

FLORINDA

Sir, let me go, I conjure you, or I'll call out.

WILLMORE

Ay, ay, you were best to call witness to see how finely you treat me. Do.

FLORINDA

I'll cry murder, rape, or anything if you do not instantly let me go!

WILLMORE

A rape! Come, come, you lie, you baggage, you lie. What, I'll warrant you would fain have the world believe now that you are not so forward as I. No, not you! – Why, at this time of night, was your cobweb door set open, dear spider, but to catch flies? Ha, come – or I shall be damnably angry. Why, what a coil is here.

FLORINDA

Sir, can you think –

38–9 *that . . . nation* Q1–3 (om. C).
56 *coil* turmoil, confusion.

WILLMORE

That you would do't for nothing? Oh, oh, I find what you would be at. – Look here, here's a pistole for you. Here's a work indeed. – Here, take it, I say.

FLORINDA

For Heaven's sake, sir, as you're a gentleman –

WILLMORE

So – now, now, she would be wheedling me for more! What, you will not take it then? You are resolved you will not? Come, come take it or I'll put it up again – for look ye, I never give more. Why, how now mistress, are you so high i'th' mouth a pistole won't down with you? Ha, why, what a work's here! – In good time. Come, no struggling to be gone. – But an y'are good at a dumb wrestle I'm for ye. Look ye, I'm for ye –

She struggles with him

Enter BELVILE *and* FREDERICK

BELVILE

The door is open; a pox of this mad fellow. I'm angry that we've lost him; I durst have sworn he had followed us.

FREDERICK

But you were so hasty, colonel, to be gone.

FLORINDA

Help! Help! Murder! Help – oh, I am ruined!

BELVILE

Ha! Sure, that's Florinda's voice. (*Comes up to them*) – A man! Villain, let go that lady.

A noise, WILLMORE *turns and draws;* FREDERICK *interposes*

FLORINDA

Belvile! Heavens! My brother, too, is coming, and 'twill be impossible to escape. – Belvile, I conjure you to walk under my chamber window, from whence I'll give you some instructions what to do. This rude man has undone us! *Exit*

WILLMORE

Belvile!

60 *pistole* See II.ii.34.

65 *up* away.

66 *high i'th'mouth* See II.ii.25 note.

67 *down* 1) go down, i.e. satisfy 2) cause you to go down, i.e. lie with me.

68 *an* if.

Enter PEDRO, STEPHANO, *and other servants, with lights*

PEDRO
I'm betrayed! Run, Stephano, and see if Florinda be safe.

Exit STEPHANO

They fight and Pedro's party beats 'em out.
[*Enter* STEPHANO]

So, whoe'er they be, all is not well. (*Going out* [*he*] *meets* STEPHANO) I'll to Florinda's chamber.

STEPHANO
You need not, sir, the poor lady's fast asleep and thinks no harm. I would not awake her, sir, for fear of frighting her with your danger.

PEDRO
I'm glad she's there. – Rascals, how came the garden door open?

STEPHANO
That question comes too late, sir – some of my fellow servants masquerading, I'll warrant.

PEDRO
Masquerading! A lewd custom to debauch our youth. There's something more in this than I imagine.

Exeunt [PEDRO *and* STEPHANO]

[ACT III, SCENE vi]

Scene changes to the street

Enter BELVILE *in rage,* FREDERICK *holding him,* *and* WILLMORE, *melancholy*

WILLMORE
Why, how the devil should I know Florinda?

BELVILE
Ah, plague of your ignorance! If it had not been Florinda, must you be a beast – a brute, a senseless swine?

WILLMORE
Well, sir, you see I am endued with patience – I can bear. Though, egad, y'are very free with me, methinks. I was in good

85 *awake* Q1, Q2, C (wake Q3).

hopes the quarrel would have been on my side, for so uncivilly interrupting me.

BELVILE

Peace, brute! Whilst thou'rt safe – oh, I'm distracted.

WILLMORE

Nay, nay, I'm an unlucky dog, that's certain.

BELVILE

Ah, curse upon the star that ruled my birth – or whatsoever other influence that makes me still so wretched!

WILLMORE

Thou break'st my heart with these complaints. There is no star in fault, no influence but sack, the cursed sack I drunk.

FREDERICK

Why, how the devil came you so drunk?

WILLMORE

Why, how the devil came you so sober?

BELVILE

A curse upon his thin skull; he was always beforehand that way.

FREDERICK

Prithee, dear colonel, forgive him; he's sorry for his fault.

BELVILE

He's always so after he has done a mischief – a plague on all such brutes!

WILLMORE

By this light, I took her for an arrant harlot.

BELVILE

Damn your debauched opinion! Tell me, sot, hadst thou so much sense and light about thee to distinguish her woman, and couldst not see something about her face and person to strike an awful reverence into thy soul?

WILLMORE

Faith, no; I considered her as mere a woman as I could wish.

BELVILE

'Sdeath, I have no patience – draw, or I'll kill you.

WILLMORE

Let that alone till tomorrow, and if I set not all right again, use your pleasure.

13 *drunk* Q1, Q3 (drank Q2, C).

16 *beforehand* ready in advance, anticipating – i.e. the opportunity to seduce a woman.

20 *arrant* See II.i.75 note.

24 *awful* respectful.

BELVILE
Tomorrow! Damn it,
The spiteful light will lead me to no happiness.
Tomorrow is Antonio's, and perhaps
Guides him to my undoing. Oh, that I could meet
This rival, this powerful fortunate!

WILLMORE
What then?

BELVILE
Let thy own reason, or my rage instruct thee.

WILLMORE
I shall be finely informed then, no doubt. Hear me, colonel, hear me. Show me the man and I'll do his business.

BELVILE
I know him no more than thou, or if I did, I should not need thy aid.

WILLMORE
This, you say, is Angellica's house. I promised the kind baggage to lie with her tonight. *Offers to go in*

Enter ANTONIO *and his* PAGE. ANTONIO *knocks on the hilt of's sword*

ANTONIO
You paid the thousand crowns I directed?

PAGE
To the lady's old woman, sir, I did.

WILLMORE
Who the devil have we here?

BELVILE
I'll now plant myself under Florinda's window, and if I find no comfort there, I'll die.

Exeunt BELVILE *and* FREDERICK

Enter MORETTA

MORETTA
Page!

PAGE
Here's my lord.

41 s.d. 2 *knocks* ed. (knock Q1).

WILLMORE

How is this? A picaroon going to board my frigate? Here's one chase gun for you.

Drawing his sword, [he] jostles ANTONIO, *who turns and draws. They fight.* ANTONIO *falls*

MORETTA

Oh, bless us! We're all undone!

Runs in and shuts the door

PAGE

Help! Murder!

Enter BELVILE *at the noise of fighting*

BELVILE

Ha! The mad rogue's engaged in some unlucky adventure again.

Enter two or three MASQUERADERS

MASQUERADER

Ha! A man killed!

WILLMORE

How? A man killed! Then I'll go home to sleep.

Puts up [his sword] and reels out.
Exeunt MASQUERADERS *another way*

BELVILE

Who should it be? Pray Heaven the rogue is safe, for all my quarrel to him.

As BELVILE *is groping about, enter an* OFFICER *and six* SOLDIERS

SOLDIER

Who's there?

OFFICER

So, here's one dispatched. Secure the murderer.

BELVILE

Do not mistake my charity for murder! I came to his assistance.

SOLDIERS *seize on* BELVILE

49 *picaroon* See II.ii.158 note.
50 *chase gun* naval gun used in pursuit
52 s.d. *Enter* BELVILE ed. (Belvile returns Q1).

OFFICER
That shall be tried, sir. – St Jago! Swords drawn in the carnival time!

Goes to ANTONIO

ANTONIO
Thy hand, prithee.

OFFICER
Ha! Don Antonio! Look well to the villain, there. – How is it, sir?

ANTONIO
I'm hurt.

BELVILE
Has my humanity made me a criminal?

OFFICER
Away with him.

BELVILE
What a cursed chance is this?

Exeunt SOLDIERS *with* BELVILE

ANTONIO (*To the* OFFICER)
This is the man that has set upon me twice. Carry him to my apartment till you have further orders from me.

Exeunt [OFFICER *and*] ANTONIO, *led*

61 *St Jago* St Iago (St James).

ACT IV, SCENE i

A fine room [with a table]

Discovers BELVILE *as by dark alone*

BELVILE

When shall I be weary of railing on fortune, who is resolved never to turn with smiles upon me? Two such defeats in one night none but the devil and that mad rogue could have contrived to have plagued me with. I am here a prisoner – but where, Heaven knows. And if there be murder done, I can soon decide the fate of a stranger in a nation without mercy. Yet this is nothing to the torture my soul bows with when I think of losing my fair, my dear Florinda. Hark, my door opens. – A light! A man – and seems of quality. Armed, too! Now shall I die like a dog without defence.

Enter ANTONIO *in a nightgown, with a light; his arm in a scarf, and a sword under his arm: he sets the candle on the table*

ANTONIO

Sir, I come to know what injuries I have done you, that could provoke you to so mean an action as to attack me basely, without allowing time for my defence?

BELVILE

Sir, for a man in my circumstances to plead innocence, would look like fear – but view me well and you will find no marks of coward on me; not anything that betrays that brutality you accuse me with.

ANTONIO

In vain, sir, you impose upon my sense. You are not only he who drew on me last night, but yesterday before the same house, that of Angellica. Yet there is something in your face and mien that makes me wish I were mistaken.

BELVILE

I own I fought today in the defence of a friend of mine with whom you, if you're the same, and your party, were first engaged.

0 s.d. 2 *as . . . alone* as if in the dark.
18–21 prose ed. (verse Q1).

Perhaps you think this crime enough to kill me, but if you do, I cannot fear you'll do it basely.

ANTONIO

No, sir, I'll make you fit for a defence with this.

Gives him the sword

BELVILE

This gallantry surprises me – nor know I how to use this present, sir, against a man so brave.

ANTONIO

You shall not need; for know, I come to snatch you from a danger that is decreed against you: perhaps your life, or long imprisonment. And 'twas with so much courage you offended, I cannot see you punished.

BELVILE

How shall I pay this generosity?

ANTONIO

It had been safer to have killed another than have attempted me. To show your danger, sir, I'll let you know my quality: and 'tis the viceroy's son whom you have wounded.

BELVILE

The viceroy's son! (*Aside*) Death and confusion! Was this plague reserved to complete all the rest? Obliged by him – the man of all the world I would destroy!

ANTONIO

You seem disordered, sir.

BELVILE

Yes, trust me, sir, I am, and 'tis with pain that man receives such bounties, who wants the power to pay 'em back again.

ANTONIO

To gallant spirits 'tis indeed uneasy; but you may quickly overpay me, sir.

BELVILE (*Aside*)

Then I am well, kind Heaven! But set us even, that I may fight with him and keep my honour safe. [*To* ANTONIO] – Oh, I'm

24 *Perhaps . . . me,* separate line in Q1.
24–5 *but . . . basely.* prose ed. (verse Q1).
25 *fear* i.e. 'fear but'.
29–67 prose ed. (verse Q1).
35 *quality* social rank.
42 *wants* See I.ii.8 note.

impatient, sir, to be discounting the mighty debt I owe you. Command me quickly.

ANTONIO

I have a quarrel with a rival, sir, about the maid we love.

BELVILE (*Aside*)

Death, 'tis Florinda he means – that thought destroys my reason, and I shall kill him!

ANTONIO

My rival, sir, is one has all the virtues man can boast of –

BELVILE (*Aside*)

Death! Who should this be?

ANTONIO

He challenged me to meet him on the Molo as soon as day appeared, but last night's quarrel has made my arm unfit to guide a sword.

BELVILE

I apprehend you, sir. You'd have me kill the man that lays a claim to the maid you speak of. I'll do't. I'll fly to do't!

ANTONIO

Sir, do you know her?

BELVILE

No, sir, but 'tis enough she is admired by you.

ANTONIO

Sir, I shall rob you of the glory on't, for you must fight under my name and dress.

BELVILE

That opinion must be strangely obliging that makes you think I can personate the brave Antonio, whom I can but strive to imitate.

ANTONIO

You say too much to my advantage. Come, sir, the day appears that calls you forth. Within, sir, is the habit. *Exit*

BELVILE

Fantastic fortune, thou deceitful light,
That cheats the wearied traveller by night,
Though on a precipice each step you tread,
I am resolved to follow where you lead. *Exit*

47 *discounting* repaying.
54 s.p. ANTONIO Q3, C2 (om. Q1).
67 *habit* clothes, i.e. to disguise him.

[ACT IV,] SCENE [ii]

The Molo

Enter FLORINDA *and* CALLIS *in masks, with* STEPHANO

FLORINDA (*Aside*)
I'm dying with my fears: Belvile's not coming as I expected under my window, makes me believe that all those fears are true. [*To* STEPHANO] – Canst thou not tell with whom my brother fights?

STEPHANO
No, madam, they were both in masquerade. I was by when they challenged one another, and they had decided the quarrel then, but were prevented by some cavaliers; which made 'em put it off till now – but I am sure 'tis about you they fight.

FLORINDA (*Aside*)
Nay, then 'tis with Belvile, for what other lover have I that dares fight for me, except Antonio, and he is too much in favour with my brother. If it be he, for whom shall I direct my prayers to Heaven?

STEPHANO
Madam, I must leave you, for if my master see me, I shall be hanged for being your conductor. I escaped narrowly for the excuse I made for you last night i'th' garden.

FLORINDA
And I'll reward thee for't. Prithee, no more.

Exit STEPHANO

Enter DON PEDRO *in his masking habit*

PEDRO
Antonio's late today; the place will fill, and we may be prevented.

Walks about

FLORINDA (*Aside*)
Antonio? Sure, I heard amiss.

1–4 prose ed. (Makes . . . true. / – Canst . . . fights? Q1).
14 *I* C2 (om. Q1–3, C).

PEDRO

But who will not excuse a happy lover
When soft, fair arms confine the yielding neck,
And the kind whisper languishingly breathes,
'Must you be gone so soon?'
Sure I had dwelt forever on her bosom –
But stay, he's here.

Enter BELVILE *dressed in Antonio's clothes*

FLORINDA (*Aside*)

'Tis not Belvile; half my fears are vanished.

PEDRO

Antonio!

BELVILE (*Aside*)

This must be he. [*To* PEDRO] – You're early, sir; I do not use to be outdone this way.

PEDRO

The wretched, sir, are watchful, and 'tis enough you've the advantage of me in Angellica.

BELVILE (*Aside*)

Angellica! Or I've mistook my man, or else Antonio! Can he forget his interest in Florinda and fight for common prize?

PEDRO

Come, sir, you know our terms.

BELVILE (*Aside*)

By Heaven, not I! [*To* PEDRO] – No talking; I am ready, sir.

[BELVILE] *offers to fight;* FLORINDA *runs in*

FLORINDA (*To* BELVILE)

Oh, hold! Whoe'er you be, I do conjure you hold! If you strike here, I die.

PEDRO

Florinda!

BELVILE

Florinda imploring for my rival!

PEDRO

Away; this kindness is unseasonable.

28–9 lineation ed. (This . . . he. / – You're . . . way. Q1).
30–1 prose ed. (verse Q1).
32 *Or . . . or* Either . . . or.

Puts her by; they fight; she runs in just as BELVILE *disarms* PEDRO

FLORINDA
Who are you, sir, that dares deny my prayers?

BELVILE
Thy prayers destroy him. If thou wouldst preserve him,
Do that thou'rt unacquainted with, and curse him.

She holds BELVILE

FLORINDA
By all you hold most dear, by her you love,
I do conjure you: touch him not.

BELVILE
By her I love!
See – I obey – and at your feet resign
The useless trophy of my victory.

Lays his sword at her feet

PEDRO
Antonio, you've done enough to prove you love Florinda.

BELVILE
Love Florinda! Does Heaven love adoration, prayer, or penitence? Love her! Here, sir, your sword again.

Snatches up the sword and gives it to him

Upon this truth I'll fight my life away.

PEDRO
No, you've redeemed my sister, and my friendship.

He gives him FLORINDA *and pulls off his vizard to show his face, and puts it on again*

BELVILE
Don Pedro!

PEDRO
Can you resign your claims to other women,
And give your heart entirely to Florinda?

BELVILE
Entire, as dying saints' confessions are!
I can delay my happiness no longer.

41 *dares* (dare Q2, C).

This minute, let me make Florinda mine!

PEDRO

This minute let it be – no time so proper!
This night my father will arrive from Rome,
And possibly may hinder what we purpose.

FLORINDA

Oh, Heavens! This minute!

Enter masqueraders and pass over [the stage]

BELVILE [*Aside*]

Oh, do not ruin me!

PEDRO

The place begins to fill, and that we may not be observed, do you walk off to St Peter's Church, where I will meet you, and conclude your happiness.

BELVILE

I'll meet you there. (*Aside*) – If there be no more saints' churches in Naples.

FLORINDA

Oh, stay, sir, and recall your hasty doom!
Alas, I have not prepared my heart
To entertain so strange a guest.

PEDRO

Away; this silly modesty is assumed too late.

BELVILE

Heaven, madam, what do you do?

FLORINDA

Do? Despise the man that lays a tyrant's claim
To what he ought to conquer by submission.

BELVILE

You do not know me – move a little this way.

Draws her aside

FLORINDA

Yes, you may force me even to the altar.
But not the holy man that offers there
Shall force me to be thine.

PEDRO *talks to* CALLIS *this while*

BELVILE

Oh, do not lose so blest an opportunity.

See – 'tis your Belvile – not Antonio
Whom your mistaken scorn and anger ruins!

Pulls off his vizard

FLORINDA
Belvile!
Where was my soul it could not meet thy voice
And take this knowledge in?

As they are talking, enter WILLMORE, *finely dressed, and* FREDERICK

WILLMORE
No intelligence? No news of Belvile yet? Well, I am the most unlucky rascal in nature. Ha! Am I deceived, or is it he? Look Fred, 'tis he – my dear Belvile.

Runs and embraces him. Belvile's vizard falls out on's hand

BELVILE
Hell and confusion seize thee!

PEDRO
Ha! Belvile! I beg your pardon, sir.

Takes FLORINDA *from him*

BELVILE
Nay, touch her not. She's mine by conquest, sir;
I won her by my sword.

WILLMORE
Didst thou so? And, egad, child, we'll keep her by the sword.

Draws on PEDRO. BELVILE *goes between* [*them*]

BELVILE
Stand off!
Thou'rt so profanely lewd, so cursed by Heaven,
All quarrels thou espousest must be fatal.

WILLMORE
Nay, an you be so hot, my valour's coy,
And shall be courted when you want it next.

87 *intelligence* tidings.
89 *Fred,* ed. (Ferd – Q1; as s.p. Q2, C, C2, with following sentence assigned).
98–9 verse ed. (prose Q1). 98 *an* See III.v.68 note.

Puts up his sword

BELVILE (*To* PEDRO)
You know I ought to claim a victor's right.
But you're the brother to divine Florinda,
To whom I'm such a slave: to purchase her
I durst not hurt the man she holds so dear.

PEDRO
'Twas by Antonio's, not by Belvile's sword
This question should have been decided, sir.
I must confess, much to your bravery's due,
Both now, and when I met you last in arms.
But I am nicely punctual in my word,
As men of honour ought, and beg your pardon.
For this mistake, another time shall clear.

Aside to FLORINDA *as they are going out*

This was some plot between you and Belvile.
But I'll prevent you.

[*Exit with* FLORINDA]

BELVILE *looks after her and begins to walk up and down in rage*

WILLMORE
Do not be modest now and lose the woman; but if we shall fetch her back so –

BELVILE
Do not speak to me!

WILLMORE
Not speak to you! Egad, I'll speak to you, and will be answered too!

BELVILE
Will you, sir!

WILLMORE
I know I've done some mischief, but I'm so dull a puppy that I'm the son of a whore if I know how, or where. Prithee, inform my understanding.

107 *when . . . arms* i.e. at the siege.
108 *nicely punctual* scrupulously definite.
110 *clear* elucidate.
118 *sir!* ed. (Sir – Q1).

BELVILE

Leave me, I say, and leave me instantly.

WILLMORE

I will not leave you in this humour, nor till I know my crime.

BELVILE

Death, I'll tell you, sir –

Draws and runs at WILLMORE, [*who*] *runs out,* BELVILE *after him;* FREDERICK *interposes* [*but does not follow them*]

Enter ANGELLICA, MORETTA, *and* SEBASTIAN

ANGELLICA

Ha! – Sebastian, is that not Willmore? Haste, haste, and bring him back.

[*Exit* SEBASTIAN]

FREDERICK

The colonel's mad: I never saw him thus before. I'll after 'em, lest he do some mischief, for I am sure Willmore will not draw on him. *Exit*

ANGELLICA

I am all rage! My first desires defeated!
For one, for aught he knows, that has no
Other merit than her quality –
Her being Don Pedro's sister. He loves her!
I know 'tis so. Dull, dull, insensible –
He will not see me now, though oft invited,
And broke his word last night – false, perjured man!
He that but yesterday fought for my favours,
And would have made his life a sacrifice
To've gained one night with me,
Must now be hired and courted to my arms.

MORETTA

I told you what would come on't, but Moretta's an old, doting fool. Why did you give him five hundred crowns, but to set himself out for other lovers? You should have kept him poor if you had meant to have had any good from him.

130 *all* Q1, Q2, C (om. Q3).
132 *quality* See IV.i.35 note.
134 *insensible* unintelligible.
142–3 *set himself out* dress himself up.

ANGELLICA

Oh, name not such mean trifles. Had I given
Him all my youth has earned from sin,
I had not lost a thought, nor sigh upon't.
But I have given him my eternal rest,
My whole repose, my future joys, my heart!
My virgin heart, Moretta! Oh, 'tis gone!

MORETTA

Curse on him, here he comes; how fine she has made him, too.

Enter WILLMORE *and* SEBASTIAN
ANGELLICA *turns and walks away*

WILLMORE

How now, turned shadow!
Fly when I pursue, and follow when I fly!

Sings

Stay, gentle shadow of my dove
And tell me ere I go,
Whether the substance may not prove
A fleeting thing like you.

As she turns, she looks on him

There's a soft, kind look remaining yet.

ANGELLICA

Well, sir, you may be gay: all happiness, all joys pursue you still. Fortune's your slave and gives you, every hour, choice of new hearts and beauties, till you are cloyed with the repeated bliss which others vainly languish for. But know, false man, that I shall be revenged.

Turns away in rage

WILLMORE

So, gad, there are of those faint-hearted lovers, whom such a sharp lesson next their hearts would make as impotent as fourscore. Pox o' this whining – my business is to laugh and love – a pox on't! I hate your sullen lover: a man shall lose as much time to put you in humour now, as would serve to gain a new woman.

145–6 *Oh, . . . Him all* (one line Q1–3, C, C2).
151 prose ed. (Curse . . . comes; / How . . . too. Q1).

ANGELLICA
I scorn to cool that fire I cannot raise,
Or do the drudgery of your virtuous mistress.

WILLMORE
A virtuous mistress! Death, what a thing thou hast found out for me! Why, what the devil should I do with a virtuous woman – a sort of ill-natured creatures, that take a pride to torment a lover? Virtue is but an infirmity in woman, a disease that renders even the handsome ungrateful; whilst the ill-favoured, for want of solicitations and address, only fancy themselves so. I have lain with a woman of quality, who has all the while been railing at whores.

ANGELLICA
I will not answer for your mistress's virtue,
Though she be young enough to know no guilt;
And I could wish you would persuade my heart
'Twas the two hundred thousand crowns you courted.

WILLMORE
Two hundred thousand crowns! What story's this? What trick? What woman? – Ha!

ANGELLICA
How strange you make it; have you forgot the creature you entertained on the Piazza last night?

WILLMORE (*Aside*)
Ha! My gipsy worth two hundred thousand crowns! Oh, how I long to be with her. Pox, I knew she was of quality.

ANGELLICA
False man! I see my ruin in thy face.
How many vows you breathed upon my bosom,
Never to be unjust. Have you forgot so soon?

WILLMORE
Faith no; I was just coming to repeat 'em. (*Aside*) – But here's a humour indeed would make a man a saint. Would she would be angry enough to leave me, and command me not to wait on her.

Enter HELLENA *dressed in man's clothes*

HELLENA [*Aside*]
This must be Angellica! I know it by her mumping matron here

186 *How . . . make it* How you affect indignation about it.
197 *mumping* grimacing, miserable.

– ay, ay, 'tis she! My mad captain's with her, too, for all his swearing. How this unconstant humour makes me love him! [*To* MORETTA] – Pray, good, grave gentlewoman, is not this Angellica?

MORETTA

My too-young-sir, it is. [*Aside*] – I hope 'tis one from Don Antonio.

Goes to ANGELLICA

HELLENA (*Aside*)

Well, something I'll do to vex him for this.

ANGELLICA

I will not speak with him; am I in humour to receive a lover?

WILLMORE

Not speak with him! Why, I'll be gone, and wait your idler minutes. Can I show less obedience to the thing I love so fondly?

Offers to go

ANGELLICA

A fine excuse this! Stay!

WILLMORE

And hinder your advantage! Should I repay your bounties so ungratefully?

ANGELLICA [*To* HELLENA]

Come hither, boy [*To* WILLMORE] – that I may let you see
How much above the advantages you name
I prize one minute's joy with you.

WILLMORE (*Impatient to be gone*)

Oh, you destroy me with this endearment.
(*Aside*) – Death! How shall I get away? – Madam, 'twill not be fit I should be seen with you. – Besides, it will not be convenient – and I've a friend – that's dangerously sick.

ANGELLICA

I see you're impatient – yet you shall stay.

WILLMORE (*Aside*)

And miss my assignation with my gipsy.

199 *unconstant* Q1, Q3 (inconstant Q2, C, C2); i.e. unfaithful in love.

Walks about impatiently. MORETTA *brings* HELLENA,
who addresses herself to ANGELLICA

HELLENA
Madam,
You'll hardly pardon my intrusion
When you shall know my business!
And I'm too young to tell my tale with art;
But there must be a wondrous store of goodness
Where so much beauty dwells.

ANGELLICA
A pretty advocate whoever sent thee.
Prithee proceed. (*To* WILLMORE *who is stealing off*)
– Nay, sir, you shall not go.

WILLMORE (*Aside*)
Then I shall lose my dear gipsy forever.
Pox on't; she stays me out of spite.

[HELLENA]
I am related to a lady, madam,
Young, rich, and nobly born, but has the fate
To be in love with a young English gentleman.
Strangely she loves him: at first sight she loved him,
But did adore him when she heard him speak;
For he, she said, had charms in every word,
That failed not to surprise, to wound and conquer.

WILLMORE (*Aside*)
Ha! Egad, I hope this concerns me.

ANGELLICA
'Tis my false man he means: would he were gone.
This praise will raise his pride, and ruin me.
(*To* WILLMORE) – Well,
Since you are so impatient to be gone,
I will release you, sir.

WILLMORE (*Aside*)
Nay, then I'm sure 'twas me he spoke of; this cannot be the effects of kindness in her.
– No, madam, I've considered better on't,
And will not give you cause of jealousy.

220 s.d. *Walks* . . . ANGELLICA ed. (*Aside, and walks* . . . *Angellica* Q1).
231 s.p. HELLENA ed. (Ang. Q1).

ANGELLICA
But, sir, I've – business that –
WILLMORE
This shall not do; I know 'tis but to try me.
ANGELLICA
Well, to your story, boy (*Aside*) – though 'twill undo me.
HELLENA
With this addition to his other beauties,
He won her unresisting, tender heart.
He vowed, and sighed, and swore he loved her dearly;
And she believed the cunning flatterer,
And thought herself the happiest maid alive.
Today was the appointed time by both
To consummate their bliss;
The virgin, altar, and the priest were dressed,
And while she languished for th'expected bridegroom,
She heard he paid his broken vows to you.
WILLMORE [*Aside*]
So, this is some dear rogue that's in love with me, and this way lets me know it; or if it be not me, he means someone whose place I may supply.
ANGELLICA
Now I perceive
The cause of thy impatience to be gone,
And all the business of this glorious dress.
WILLMORE
Damn the young prater; I know not what he means.
HELLENA
Madam,
In your fair eyes I read too much concern
To tell my farther business.
ANGELLICA
Prithee, sweet youth, talk on; thou may'st perhaps
Raise here a storm that may undo my passion,
And then I'll grant thee anything.
HELLENA
Madam, 'tis to entreat you (oh, unreasonable!)
You would not see this stranger;

260 s.d. *Aside* C2 (om. Q1–3, C).
260–1 prose ed. (verse Q1).
266 *prater* idle chatterer.

For if you do, she vows you are undone,
Though nature never made a man so excellent,
And sure, he 'ad been a god, but for inconstancy.

WILLMORE (*Aside*)
Ah, rogue, how finely he's instructed!
'Tis plain; some woman that has seen me *en passant.*

ANGELLICA
Oh, I shall burst with jealousy! Do you know the man you speak of?

HELLENA
Yes, madam; he used to be in buff and scarlet.

ANGELLICA (*To* WILLMORE)
Thou, false as Hell, what canst thou say to this?

WILLMORE
By Heaven –

ANGELLICA
Hold, do not damn thyself –

HELLENA
Nor hope to be believed.

He walks about; they follow

ANGELLICA
Oh, perjured man!
Is't thus you pay my generous passion back?

HELLENA
Why would you, sir, abuse my lady's faith?

ANGELLICA
And use me so inhumanely.

HELLENA
A maid so young, so innocent –

WILLMORE
Ah, young devil.

ANGELLICA
Dost thou not know thy life is in my power?

HELLENA
Or think my lady cannot be revenged?

279 *en passant* in passing.
290 *inhumanely* Q2, Q3, C, C2 (unhumanely Q1).
292 *devil* ed. (Divel Q1).
293 *in my* Q2, Q3, C, C2 (my Q1).

WILLMORE (*Aside*)
So, so, the storm comes finely on.

ANGELLICA
Now thou art silent; guilt has struck thee dumb.
Oh, hadst thou still been so, I'd lived in safety.

She turns away and weeps

WILLMORE (*Aside to* HELLENA)
Sweet heart, the lady's name and house – quickly!
I'm impatient to be with her.

Looks towards ANGELLICA *to watch her turning, and as she comes towards them, he meets her*

HELLENA (*Aside*)
So, now is he for another woman.

WILLMORE
The impudent'st young thing in nature,
I cannot persuade him out of his error, madam.

ANGELLICA
I know he's in the right – yet thou'st a tongue
That would persuade him to deny his faith.

In rage walks away

WILLMORE (*Said softly to* HELLENA)
Her name, her name, dear boy –

HELLENA
Have you forgot it, sir?

WILLMORE (*Aside*)
Oh, I perceive he's not to know I am a stranger to his lady.
– Yes, yes, I do know, but I have forgot the –

(ANGELLICA *turns*)

– By Heaven, such early confidence I never saw.

ANGELLICA
Did I not charge you with this mistress, sir?
Which you denied, though I beheld your perjury.
This little generosity of thine has rendered back my heart.

Walks away

297 *still* always (*OED* 7b).
301 *impudent'st* ed. (impudents Q1).

WILLMORE [*To* HELLENA]
So, you have made sweet work here, my little mischief; look your lady be kind and good natured now, or I shall have but a cursed bargain on't.

(ANGELLICA *turns towards them*)

– The rogue's bred up to mischief;
Art thou so great a fool to credit him?

ANGELLICA
Yes, I do, and you in vain impose upon me.
[*To* HELLENA] – Come hither, boy. Is not this he you spake of?

HELLENA
I think – it is; I cannot swear, but I vow he has just such another lying lover's look.

HELLENA *looks in his face; he gazes on her*

WILLMORE
Ha! Do not I know that face?
(*Aside*) – By Heaven, my little gipsy! What a dull dog was I. Had I but looked that way, I'd known her. Are all my hopes of a new woman banished? [*To* HELLENA] – Egad, if I do not fit thee for this, hang me. [*To* ANGELLICA] – Madam, I have found out the plot.

HELLENA [*Aside*]
Oh lord, what does he say? Am I discovered now?

WILLMORE
Do you see this young spark here?

HELLENA [*Aside*]
He'll tell her who I am.

WILLMORE
Who do you think this is?

HELLENA [*Aside*]
Ay, ay, he does know me. [*To* WILLMORE] – Nay, dear captain! I am undone if you discover me.

WILLMORE
Nay, nay, no cogging. She shall know what a precious mistress I have.

313–17 verse in Q1.
319 *spake* Q1 (speak Q2, Q3, C, C2).
334 *cogging* wheedling.

HELLENA

Will you be such a devil?

WILLMORE

Nay, nay, I'll teach you to spoil sport you will not make. [*To* ANGELLICA] – This small ambassador comes not from a person of quality as you imagine, and he says – but from a very arrant gipsy, the talking'st, prating'st, canting'st little animal thou ever saw'st.

ANGELLICA

What news you tell me; that's the thing I mean.

HELLENA (*Aside*)

Would I were well off the place; if ever I go a-captain-hunting again –

WILLMORE

Mean that thing? That gipsy thing? Thou may'st as well be jealous of thy monkey or parrot as of her. A German motion were worth a dozen of her, and a dream were a better enjoyment – a creature of a constitution fitter for Heaven than man.

HELLENA (*Aside*)

Though I'm sure he lies, yet this vexes me.

ANGELLICA

You are mistaken; she's a Spanish woman
Made up of no such dull materials.

WILLMORE

Materials! Egad, an she be made of any that will either dispense or admit of love, I'll be bound to continence.

HELLENA (*Aside to him*)

Unreasonable man, do you think so?

[WILLMORE] (*To* HELLENA)

You may return, my little brazen head, and tell your lady that till she be handsome enough to be beloved, or I dull enough to be religious, there will be small hopes of me.

ANGELLICA

Did you not promise, then, to marry her?

WILLMORE

Not I, by Heaven.

340 *arrant* See II.i.75 note.
346 *motion* puppet (i.e. automaton).
353 *continence* restraint in relation to sexual appetite.
355 s.p. *WILLMORE* Q3, C, C2 (om. Q1, Q2).

ANGELLICA
You cannot undeceive my fears and torments till you have vowed you will not marry her.

HELLENA (*Aside*)
If he swears that, he'll be revenged on me indeed for all my rogueries.

ANGELLICA
I know what arguments you'll bring against me – fortune, and honour.

WILLMORE
Honour! I tell you, I hate it in your sex; and those that fancy themselves possessed of that foppery are the most impertinently troublesome of all womankind, and will transgress nine commandments to keep one, and to satisfy your jealousy, I swear –

HELLENA (*Aside to him*)
Oh, no swearing, dear captain.

WILLMORE
If it were possible I should ever be inclined to marry, it should be some kind young sinner; one that has generosity enough to give a favour handsomely to one that can ask it discreetly; one that has wit enough to manage an intrigue or love. Oh, how civil such a wench is to a man that does her the honour to marry her.

ANGELLICA
By Heaven there's no faith in anything he says.

Enter SEBASTIAN

SEBASTIAN
Madam, Don Antonio –

ANGELLICA
Come hither.

HELLENA [*Aside*]
Ha! Antonio! He may be coming hither and he'll certainly discover me; I'll therefore retire without a ceremony. *Exit*

ANGELLICA
I'll see him; get my coach ready.

HELLENA
It waits you, madam.

362 *swears that,* ed. (Swears, that Q1).

WILLMORE [*Aside*]

This is lucky. – What, madam, now I may be gone and leave you to the enjoyment of my rival?

ANGELLICA

Dull man, that canst not see how ill, how poor,
That false dissimulation looks. Begone
And never let me see thy cozening face again,
Lest I relapse and kill thee.

WILLMORE

Yes, you can spare me now. Farewell, till you're in better humour. [*Aside*] – I'm glad of this release.
Now for my gipsy:
For though to worse we change, yet still we find
New joys, new charms, in a new miss that's kind. *Exit*

ANGELLICA

He's gone, and in this ague of my soul
The shivering fit returns.
Oh, with what willing haste he took his leave,
As if the longed-for minute were arrived
Of some blest assignation.
In vain I have consulted all my charms,
In vain this beauty prized, in vain believed
My eyes could kindle any lasting fires;
I had forgot my name, my infamy,
And the reproach that honour lays on those
That dare pretend a sober passion here.
Nice reputation, though it leave behind
More virtues than inhabit where that dwells;
Yet that once gone, those virtues shine no more.
Then since I am not fit to be beloved,
I am resolved to think on a revenge
On him that soothed me thus to my undoing.

Exeunt [SEBASTIAN *and* ANGELLICA]

389 *cozening* deceitful.
407 *Nice* 1) strict, scrupulous 2) delicate.
412 *soothed* flattered, cajoled.

[ACT IV,] SCENE iii

A street

Enter FLORINDA *and* VALERIA *in habits different from what they have been seen in*

FLORINDA

We're happily escaped, and yet I tremble still.

VALERIA

A lover and fear! Why, I am but half an one, and yet I have courage for any attempt. Would Hellena were here; I would fain have had her as deep in this mischief as we. She'll fare but ill else, I doubt.

FLORINDA

She pretended a visit to the Augustine nuns, but I believe some other design carried her out; pray Heaven we light on her. Prithee what didst do with Callis?

VALERIA

When I saw no reason would do good on her, I followed her into the wardrobe, and as she was looking for something in a great chest, I toppled her in by the heels, snatched the key of the apartment where you were confined, locked her in, and left her bawling for help.

FLORINDA

'Tis well you resolve to follow my fortunes, for thou darest never appear at home again after such an action.

VALERIA

That's according as the young stranger and I shall agree. But to our business. I delivered your letter, your note to Belvile, when I got out under pretence of going to mass. I found him at his lodging, and believe me it came seasonably, for never was man in so desperate a condition. I told him of your resolution of making your escape today, if your brother would be absent long enough to permit you; if not, to die rather than be Antonio's.

FLORINDA

Thou should'st have told him I was confined to my chamber

6 *Augustine nuns* a Roman Catholic order, following the rule of St Augustine.

8 *didst* i.e. didst thou.

10 *wardrobe* dressing-room where clothing and costly objects were kept.

17 *your letter, your note* Q1–3, C, C2; but some copies of Q1 give 'your note'.

upon my brother's suspicion that the business on the Molo was a plot laid between him and I.

VALERIA

I said all this, and told him your brother was now gone to his devotion, and he resolves to visit every church till he find him, and not only undeceive him in that, but caress him so as shall delay his return home.

FLORINDA

Oh, Heavens! He's here, and Belvile with him too.

They put on their vizards

Enter DON PEDRO, BELVILE, WILLMORE; BELVILE *and* DON PEDRO *seeming in serious discourse*

VALERIA

Walk boldly by them, and I'll come at distance, lest he suspect us.

She walks by them and looks back on them

WILLMORE

Ha! A woman, and of an excellent mien.

PEDRO

She throws a kind look back on you.

WILLMORE

Death! 'Tis a likely wench, and that kind look shall not be cast away. I'll follow her.

BELVILE

Prithee do not.

WILLMORE

Do not? By Heavens, to the antipodes, with such an invitation.

[VALERIA] *goes out and* WILLMORE *follows her*

BELVILE

'Tis a mad fellow for a wench.

Enter FREDERICK

FREDERICK

Oh, colonel, such news!

24 *Molo* See II.i.200 note.
30 s.d. 1 *vizards* See II.i.0 s.d. 3 note.
33 *mien* 1) bearing 2) appearance.
38 *Do not?* (Do not, Q1).
antipodes the opposite side of the earth.

BELVILE

Prithee what?

FREDERICK

News that will make you laugh in spite of fortune.

BELVILE

What, Blunt has had some damned trick put upon him – cheated, banged, or clapped?

FREDERICK

Cheated sir, rarely cheated of all but his shirt and drawers; the unconscionable whore, too, turned him out before consummation, so that, traversing the streets at midnight, the watch found him in this *fresco*, and conducted him home. By Heaven, 'tis such a sight, and yet I durst as well been hanged as laughed at him, or pity him; he beats all that do but ask him a question, and is in such an humour.

PEDRO

Who is't has met with this ill usage, sir?

BELVILE

A friend of ours whom you must see for mirth's sake. (*Aside*) – I'll employ him to give Florinda time for an escape.

PEDRO

What is he?

BELVILE

A young countryman of ours, one that has been educated at so plentiful a rate, he yet ne'er knew the want of money; and 'twill be a great jest to see how simply he'll look without it. For my part, I'll lend him none; and the rogue know not how to put on a borrowing face and ask first, I'll let him see how good 'tis to play our parts whilst I play his. – Prithee, Fred, do you go home and keep him in that posture till we come.

Exeunt [BELVILE, DON PEDRO, *and* FREDERICK]

Enter FLORINDA *from the farther end of the scene, looking behind her*

FLORINDA

I am followed still. Ha! My brother, too, advancing this way. Good Heavens defend me from being seen by him.

She goes off

44 *banged, or clapped* violently beaten, or infected with gonorrhea.
45 *rarely* uncommonly, exceptionally.
48 *fresco* See III.i.92 note.

Enter WILLMORE, *and after him,* VALERIA, *at a little distance*

WILLMORE

Ah! There she sails! She looks back as she were willing to be boarded; I'll warrant her prize.

He goes out, VALERIA *following*

Enter HELLENA, *just as he goes out, with a* PAGE

HELLENA

Ha! Is not that my captain that has a woman in chase? 'Tis not Angellica. [*To* PAGE] – Boy, follow those people at a distance, and bring me an account where they go in.

Exit PAGE

[*Aside*] – I'll find his haunts and plague him everywhere. Ha! My brother!

BELVILE, WILLMORE, [*and*] PEDRO *cross the stage;* HELLENA *runs off*

[ACT IV, SCENE iv]

Scene changes to another street

Enter FLORINDA

FLORINDA

What shall I do? My brother now pursues me. Will no kind power protect me from his tyranny? – Ha, here's a door open; I'll venture in, since nothing can be worse than to fall into his hands. My life and honour are at stake, and my necessity has no choice. *Goes in*

Enter VALERIA *and Hellena's* PAGE, *peeping after* FLORINDA

PAGE

Here she went in; I shall remember this house.

Exit BOY

66 *warrant her prize* guarantee she's a ship I can legally capture (seize).

VALERIA

This is Belvile's lodging; she's gone in as readily as if she knew it. Ha! Here's that mad fellow again; I dare not venture in. I'll watch my opportunity. *Goes aside*

Enter WILLMORE *gazing about him*

WILLMORE

I have lost her hereabouts. Pox on't, she must not 'scape me so. *Goes out*

[ACT IV, SCENE v]

Scene changes to Blunt's chamber, discovers him sitting on a couch in his shirt and drawers, reading

BLUNT

So, now my mind's a little at peace, since I have resolved revenge. A pox on this tailor, though, for not bringing home the clothes I bespoke. And a pox of all poor cavaliers; a man can never keep a spare suit for 'em, and I shall have these rogues come in and find me naked, and then I'm undone. But I'm resolved to arm myself – the rascals shall not insult over me too much. (*Puts on an old rusty sword and buff belt*) – Now, how like a morris dancer I am equipped! A fine ladylike whore to cheat me thus, without affording me a kindness for my money – a pox light on her. I shall never be reconciled to the sex more; she has made me as faithless as a physician, as uncharitable as a churchman, and as ill-natured as a poet. Oh, how I'll use all womankind hereafter! What would I give to have one of 'em within my reach now! Any mortal thing in petticoats, kind fortune, send me, and I'll forgive thy last night's malice. – Here's a cursed book, too – 'A warning to all young travellers': that can instruct me how to prevent such mischief now 'tis too late! Well, 'tis a rare convenient thing to read a little now and then, as well as hawk and hunt.

0 s.d. 1 *discovers* See I.ii.202 note.

8 *morris dancer . . . equipped* i.e. how fantastically or grotesquely dressed I am.

16 *book* the one he was reading when the scene opened.

Sits down again and reads
Enter to him FLORINDA

FLORINDA
This house is haunted sure; 'tis well furnished and no living thing inhabits it. Ha! – A man! Heavens, how he's attired! Sure 'tis some rope-dancer or fencing master. I tremble now for fear, and yet I must venture now to speak to him. – Sir, if I may not interrupt your meditations –

He starts up and gazes

BLUNT
Ha, what's here? Are my wishes granted? And is not that a she creature? 'Adsheartlikins, 'tis! What wretched thing art thou, ha?

FLORINDA
Charitable sir, you've told yourself already what I am; a very wretched maid, forced by a strange unlucky accident to seek a safety here, and must be ruined if you do not grant it.

BLUNT
Ruined! Is there any ruin so inevitable as that which now threatens thee? Dost thou know, miserable woman, into what den of mischiefs thou art fallen? What abyss of confusion, ha? Dost not see something in my looks that frights thy guilty soul, and makes thee wish to change that shape of woman for any humble animal, or devil? For those were safer for thee, and less mischievous.

FLORINDA
Alas, what mean you, sir? I must confess, your looks have something in 'em makes me fear, but I beseech you, as you seem a gentleman, pity a harmless virgin that takes your house for sanctuary.

BLUNT
Talk on, talk on, and weep too, till my faith return. Do, flatter me out of my senses again – a harmless virgin with a pox; as much one as t'other, 'adsheartlikins. Why, what the devil, can I not be safe in my house for you, not in my chamber? Nay, even being naked, too, cannot secure me: this is an impudence greater than has invaded me yet. – Come, no resistance.

Pulls her rudely

24 s.d. *He* Q3, C, C2 (She Q1, Q2).
29 *and . . . it* verse in Q1.

FLORINDA

Dare you be so cruel?

BLUNT

Cruel, 'adsheartlikins, as a galley slave, or a Spanish whore. Cruel? Yes, I will kiss and beat thee all over; kiss and see thee all over; thou shalt lie with me too – not that I care for the enjoyment, but to let thee see I have ta'en deliberated malice to thee, and will be revenged on one whore for the sins of another. I will smile and deceive thee, flatter thee and beat thee, kiss and swear, and lie to thee, embrace thee and rob thee, as she did me, fawn on thee, and strip thee stark naked; then hang thee out at my window by the heels, with a paper of scurvy verses fastened to thy breast in praise of damnable women. – Come, come along!

FLORINDA

Alas, sir, must I be sacrificed for the crimes of the most infamous of my sex? I never understood the sins you name.

BLUNT

Do, persuade the fool you love him, or that one of you can be just or honest; tell me I was not an easy coxcomb, or any strange, impossible tale: it will be believed sooner than thy false showers or protestations. A generation of damned hypocrites to flatter my very clothes from my back! Dissembling witches! Are these the returns you make an honest gentleman that trusts, believes, and loves you? But if I be not even with you. – Come along – or I shall –

Pulls her again

Enter FREDERICK

FREDERICK

Ha! What's here to do?

BLUNT

'Adsheartlikins, Fred, I am glad thou art come, to be a witness of my dire revenge.

FREDERICK

What's this, a person of quality too, who is upon the ramble to supply the defects of some grave impotent husband?

BLUNT

No, this has another pretence; some very unfortunate accident

51 *ta'en* C2 ('tain' Q1, Q2, C; 'tame' some copies Q1; 'taken' Q3).

62 *coxcomb* See I.i.109 note.

brought her hither, to save a life pursued by I know not who, or why, and forced to take sanctuary here at Fool's Haven. 'Adsheartlikins, to me of all mankind for protection? Is the ass to be cajoled again, think ye? No, young one, no prayers or tears shall mitigate my rage; therefore prepare for both my pleasures of enjoyment and revenge, for I am resolved to make up my loss here on thy body. I'll take it out in kindness and in beating.

FREDERICK

Now, mistress of mine, what do you think of this?

FLORINDA

I think he will not – dares not be so barbarous.

FREDERICK

Have a care, Blunt, she fetched a deep sigh. She is enamoured with thy shirt and drawers; she'll strip thee even of that. There are, of her calling, such unconscionable baggages, and such dexterous thieves, they'll flay a man and he shall ne'er miss his skin till he feels the cold. There was a countryman of ours robbed of a row of teeth whilst he was a-sleeping, which the jilt made him buy again when he waked. – You see, lady, how little reason we have to trust you.

BLUNT

'Dsheartlikins, why this is most abominable.

FLORINDA

Some such devils there may be, but by all that's holy, I am none such; I entered here to save a life in danger.

BLUNT

For no goodness, I'll warrant her.

FREDERICK

Faith, damsel, you had e'en confessed the plain truth, for we are fellows not to be caught twice in the same trap. Look on that wreck, a tight vessel when he set out of haven, well-trimmed and laden, and see how a female picaroon of this island of rogues has shattered him, and canst thou hope for any mercy?

BLUNT

No, no, gentlewoman, come along. 'Adsheartlikins, we must be

79 *pleasures* Q1–3 (pleasure C, C2).
87 *flay* ed. (flea Q1).
89 *a–sleeping* Q1, Q2, C (sleeping Q3, C2).
96 *confessed* Q1, Q2 (confess Q3, C, C2).
98 *tight* water-tight.
99 *picaroon* See II.ii.158 note.

better acquainted. [*To* FREDERICK] – We'll both lie with her, and then let me alone to bang her.

FREDERICK

I'm ready to serve you in matters of revenge that has a double pleasure in't.

BLUNT

Well said. You hear, little one, how you are condemned by public vote to the bed within; there's no resisting your destiny, sweetheart.

Pulls her

FLORINDA

Stay, sir. I have seen you with Belvile, an English cavalier; for his sake use me kindly. You know him, sir.

BLUNT

Belvile? Why yes, sweeting, we do know Belvile, and wish he were with us now. He's a cormorant at whore and bacon; he'd have a limb or two of thee, my virgin pullet. But 'tis no matter; we'll leave him the bones to pick.

FLORINDA

Sir, if you have any esteem for that Belvile, I conjure you to treat me with more gentleness; he'll thank you for the justice.

FREDERICK

Hark'ee, Blunt, I doubt we are mistaken in this matter.

FLORINDA

Sir, if you find me not worth Belvile's care, use me as you please, and that you may think I merit better treatment than you threaten, pray take this present –

Gives him a ring; he looks on it

BLUNT

Hum – a diamond! Why, 'tis a wonderful virtue now that lies in this ring, a mollifying virtue. 'Adsheartlikins, there's more persuasive rhetoric in't than all her sex can utter.

FREDERICK

I begin to suspect something; and 'twould anger us vilely to be

103 *bang* See I.ii.273 note.
104–5 *has . . . in't* i.e. have . . . in them.
112 *cormorant . . . bacon* insatiably greedy devourer of whores and flesh.

trussed up for a rape upon a maid of quality, when we only believe we ruffle a harlot.

BLUNT

Thou art a credulous fellow, but 'adsheartlikins I have no faith yet. Why, my saint prattled as parlously as this does; she gave me a bracelet, too – a devil on her – but I sent my man to sell it today for necessaries, and it proved as counterfeit as her vows of love.

FREDERICK

However, let it reprieve her till we see Belvile.

BLUNT

That's hard, yet I will grant it.

Enter a SERVANT

SERVANT

Oh, sir, the colonel is just come in with his new friend and a Spaniard of quality, and talks of having you to dinner with 'em.

BLUNT

'Dsheartlikins, I'm undone – I would not see 'em for the world. Hark'ee, Fred, lock up the wench in your chamber.

FREDERICK

Fear nothing, madam; whate'er he threatens, you are safe whilst in my hands.

Exeunt FREDERICK *and* FLORINDA

BLUNT

And, sirrah, upon your life, say – I am not at home – or that I am asleep – or – or anything. Away; I'll prevent their coming this way.

Locks the door, and exeunt

126 *ruffle* handle with rude familiarity.
128 *parlously* See I.ii.140 note.

ACT V, SCENE i

Blunt's chamber

After a great knocking at his chamber door, enter BLUNT *softly crossing the stage, in his shirt and drawers as before*

[VOICES] (*Call within*)
Ned, Ned Blunt, Ned Blunt!

BLUNT
The rogues are up in arms. 'Sheartlikins, this villainous Frederick has betrayed me; they have heard of my blessed fortune.

[VOICES] (*And knocking within*)
Ned Blunt! Ned, Ned –

BELVILE [*Within*]
Why, he's dead, sir, without dispute, dead. He has not been seen today. Let's break open the door. Here, boy –

BLUNT
Ha, break open the door. 'Dsheartlikins, that mad fellow will be as good as his word.

BELVILE [*Within*]
Boy, bring something to force the door.

A great noise within, at the door again

BLUNT
So, now must I speak in my own defence; I'll try what rhetoric will do. [*To those without*] Hold, hold! What do you mean, gentlemen? What do you mean?

BELVILE (*Within*)
Oh, rogue, art alive? Prithee open the door and convince us.

BLUNT
Yes, I am alive, gentlemen – but at present a little busy.

BELVILE (*Within*)
How? Blunt grown a man of business? Come, come, open and let's see this miracle.

0 s.d. 1 *chamber* Q1–3 (room C, C2); see I.i.0 s.d. note.
1 s.p. VOICES ed. (not in Q1).
4 s.p. VOICES ed. (not in Q1).
s.d. *and knocking* Q1, Q2, C, C2 (calling and knocking Q3).

BLUNT

No, no, no, no! Gentlemen, 'tis no great business – but – I am – at – my devotion. 'Dsheartlikins, will you not allow a man time to pray?

BELVILE (*Within*)

Turned religious! A greater wonder than the first, therefore open quickly, or we shall unhinge, we shall.

BLUNT [*Aside*]

This won't do. [*To them*] – Why, hark'ee colonel, to tell you the plain truth, I am about a necessary affair of life – I have a wench with me. You apprehend me? [*Aside*] The devil's in't if they be so uncivil as to disturb me now.

WILLMORE [*Within*]

How, a wench? Nay, then we must enter and partake no resistance – unless it be your lady of quality, and then we'll keep our distance.

BLUNT [*Aside*]

So, the business is out.

WILLMORE [*Within*]

Come, come, lend's more hands to the door. – Now heave all together. (*Breaks open the door*) So, well done, my boys!

Enter BELVILE [*and his* PAGE], WILLMORE, FREDERICK, *and* PEDRO. BLUNT *looks simply; they all laugh at him. He lays his hand on his sword and comes up to* WILLMORE

BLUNT

Hark'ee, sir, laugh out your laugh quickly, d'ye hear, and begone. I shall spoil your sport else. 'Adsheartlikins, sir, I shall – the jest has been carried on too long. (*Aside*) A plague upon my tailor!

WILLMORE

'Sdeath, how the whore has dressed him! Faith sir, I'm sorry.

BLUNT

Are you so, sir? Keep't to yourself then, sir, I advise you, d'ye hear, for I can as little endure your pity as his mirth.

Lays his hand on's sword

17 *No, no, no, no* Q1, Q2, C, C2 (No, no, no Q3).
30 *lend's* i.e. lend us Q1–3, C (lend C2).
31 s.d. 2 *simply* foolishly.
32 *d'ye* (de ye Q1) The form has been changed throughout.
36 *Faith* i.e. in faith.

BELVILE
Indeed, Willmore, thou wert a little too rough with Ned Blunt's mistress. Call a person of quality, whore? And one so young, so handsome, and so eloquent – ha, ha, he.

BLUNT
Hark'ee, sir, you know me, and know I can be angry. Have a care, for 'adsheartlikins, I can fight too – I can, sir. Do you mark me? No more.

BELVILE
Why so peevish, good Ned? Some disappointments, I'll warrant. What, did the jealous count, her husband, return just in the nick?

BLUNT
Or the devil, sir. (*They laugh*) – D'ye laugh? Look ye settle me a good sober countenance, and that quickly too, or you shall know Ned Blunt is not –

BELVILE
Not everybody; we know that.

BLUNT
Not an ass to be laughed at, sir.

WILLMORE
Unconscionable sinner, to bring a lover so near his happiness – a vigorous passionate lover – and then not only cheat him of his movables, but his very desires, too!

BELVILE
Ah! Sir, a mistress is a trifle with Blunt. He'll have a dozen the next time he looks abroad. His eyes have charms not to be resisted; there needs no more than to expose that taking person to the view of the fair, and he leads 'em all in triumph.

PEDRO
Sir, though I'm a stranger to you, I am ashamed at the rudeness of my nation, and could you learn who did it, would assist you to make an example of 'em.

BLUNT
Why, ay, there's one speaks sense now, and handsomely; and let me tell you, gentlemen, I should not have showed myself like a jack pudding, thus to have made you mirth, but that I have revenge within my power. For know, I have got into my possession a female who had better have fallen under any curse than

41 *Ha, ha, he* Q1, Q2, C, C2 (Ha, ha, ha Q3).
65 *jack pudding* buffoon, clown.

the ruin I design her. 'Adsheartlikins, she assaulted me here in my own lodgings, and had doubtless committed a rape upon me, had not this sword defended me.

FREDERICK

I know not that, but o' my conscience thou had ravished her, had she not redeemed herself with a ring. Let's see it, Blunt.

BLUNT *shows the ring*

BELVILE [*Aside*]

Ha! The ring I gave Florinda when we exchanged our vows. – Hark'ee, Blunt – *Goes to whisper to him*

WILLMORE

No whispering, good colonel. There's a woman in the case, no whispering.

BELVILE [*To* BLUNT]

Hark'ee, fool, be advised, and conceal both the ring and the story for your reputation's sake. Do not let people know what despised cullies we English are; to be cheated and abused by one whore, and another rather bribe thee than be kind to thee, is an infamy to our nation.

WILLMORE

Come, come, where's the wench? We'll see her; let her be what she will, we'll see her.

PEDRO

Ay, ay, let us see her. I can soon discover whether she be of quality, or for your diversion.

BLUNT

She's in Fred's custody.

WILLMORE [*To* FREDERICK]

Come, come, the key –

[FREDERICK] *gives him the key; they are going*

BELVILE [*Aside*]

Death, what shall I do? – Stay, gentlemen. [*Aside*] – Yet if I hinder 'em I shall discover all. [*To them*] – Hold, let's go one at once. Give me the key.

72 *had* Q1, Q2 (hadst Q3, C, C2).
73 *exchanged* Q2, Q3, C, C2 (exchange Q1).
79 *cullies* See III.iv.24 note. 85 *quality* See I.ii.298 note.
89 *discover* See I.ii.202 note.
89 *let's go one* Q1, Q2, C, C2 (let one go Q3).
89–90 *one at once* one at a time.

WILLMORE

Nay, hold there, colonel. I'll go first.

FREDERICK

Nay, no dispute; Ned and I have the propriety of her.

WILLMORE

Damn propriety – then we'll draw cuts. (BELVILE *goes to whisper* [*to*] WILLMORE) – Nay, no corruption, good colonel. Come, the longest sword carries her.

They all draw, forgetting DON PEDRO, *being a Spaniard, had the longest*

BLUNT

I yield up my int'rest to you, gentlemen, and that will be revenge sufficient.

WILLMORE (*To* PEDRO)

The wench is yours. [*Aside*] – Pox of his Toledo, I had forgot that.

FREDERICK

Come, sir, I'll conduct you to the lady.

Exeunt FREDERICK *and* PEDRO

BELVILE (*Aside*)

To hinder him will certainly discover her. [*To*] WILLMORE [*who is*] *walking up and down out of humour* – Dost know, dull beast, what mischief thou hast done?

WILLMORE

Ay, ay, to trust our fortune to lots! A devil on't; 'twas madness, that's the truth on't.

BELVILE

Oh, intolerable sot –

Enter FLORINDA *running, masked,* PEDRO *after her:* WILLMORE *gazing round her*

FLORINDA (*Aside*)

Good Heaven defend me from discovery.

PEDRO

'Tis but in vain to fly me; you're fallen to my lot.

92 *propriety* Q2, Q3, C (property C2; gropriety Q1).
95 s.d. 1 *being* Q2, C, C2 (being as Q1, Q3).
96 *be* ed. (be; Q1).
98 *Toledo* a finely-tempered (and in this case, long) sword blade.
101 s.d. *To* WILLMORE Q3 (Willmore Q1, Q2, C, C2).

BELVILE

Sure, she's undiscovered yet, but now I fear there is no way to bring her off.

WILLMORE

Why, what a pox; is not this my woman? The same I followed but now?

PEDRO *talking to* FLORINDA, *who walks up and down*

PEDRO

As if I did not know ye, and your business here.

FLORINDA (*Aside*)

Good Heaven, I fear he does indeed –

PEDRO

Come, pray be kind. I know you meant to be so when you entered here, for these are proper gentlemen.

WILLMORE

But sir – perhaps the lady will not be imposed upon. She'll choose her man.

PEDRO

I am better bred than not to leave her choice free.

Enter VALERIA, *and is surprised at sight of* DON PEDRO

VALERIA (*Aside*)

Don Pedro here! There's no avoiding him.

FLORINDA (*Aside*)

Valeria! Then I'm undone –

VALERIA (*To* PEDRO, *running to him*)

Oh, have I found you, sir! The strangest accident – if I had breath – to tell it.

PEDRO

Speak! Is Florinda safe? Hellena well?

VALERIA

Ay, ay, sir. Florinda – is safe [*Aside*] – from any fears of you.

PEDRO

Why, where's Florinda? Speak.

VALERIA

Ay, where indeed, sir. I wish I could inform you – but to hold you no longer in doubt –

110 *bring her off* procure her escape.
116 *proper* See I.i.36 note.

FLORINDA (*Aside*)
Oh, what will she say?

VALERIA
She's fled away in the habit – of one of her pages, sir – but Callis thinks you may retrieve her yet, if you make haste away. She'll tell you, sir, the rest (*Aside*) – if you can find her out.

PEDRO
Dishonourable girl! She has undone my aim. [*To* BELVILE] – Sir, you see my necessity of leaving you, and hope you'll pardon it. My sister, I know, will make her flight to you; and if she do, I shall expect she should be rendered back.

BELVILE
I shall consult my love and honour, sir.

Exit PEDRO

FLORINDA (*To* VALERIA)
My dear preserver, let me embrace thee.

WILLMORE
What the devil's all this?

BLUNT
Mystery by this light.

VALERIA
Come, come, make haste and get yourselves married quickly, for your brother will return again.

BELVILE
I'm so surprised with fears and joys, so amazed to find you here in safety, I can scarce persuade my heart into a faith of what I see.

WILLMORE
Hark'ee, colonel, is this that mistress who has cost you so many sighs, and me so many quarrels with you?

BELVILE
It is. (*To* FLORINDA) Pray give him the honour of your hand.

WILLMORE
Thus it must be received then.

Kneels and kisses her hand

And with it give your pardon too.

FLORINDA
The friend to Belvile may command me anything.

134 *hope* Q1, Q3 (I hope Q2, C, C2).

WILLMORE (*Aside*)
Death, would I might! 'Tis a surprising beauty.

BELVILE
Boy, run and fetch a Father instantly.

Exit BOY

FREDERICK
So, now do I stand like a dog, and have not a syllable to plead my own cause with. By this hand, madam, I was never thoroughly confounded before, nor shall I ever more dare look up with confidence, till you are pleased to pardon me.

FLORINDA
Sir, I'll be reconciled to you on one condition – that you'll follow the example of your friend in marrying a maid that does not hate you, and whose fortune (I believe) will not be unwelcome to you.

FREDERICK
Madam, had I no inclinations that way, I should obey your kind commands.

BELVILE
Who, Fred, marry? He has so few inclinations for womankind, that had he been possessed of paradise, he might have continued there to this day, if no crime but love could have disinherited him.

FREDERICK
Oh, I do not use to boast of my intrigues.

BELVILE
Boast! Why, thou dost nothing but boast; and I dare swear, wert thou as innocent from the sin of the grape as thou art from the apple, thou might'st yet claim that right in Eden which our first parents lost by too much loving.

FREDERICK
I wish this lady would think me so modest a man.

VALERIA
She would be sorry then, and not like you half so well, and I should be loath to break my word with you, which was, that if your friend and mine agreed, it should be a match between you and I.

She gives him her hand

FREDERICK
Bear witness, colonel, 'tis a bargain. *Kisses her hand*

BLUNT (*To* FLORINDA)

I have a pardon to beg, too, but 'adsheartlikins, I am so out of countenance that I'm a dog if I can say anything to purpose.

FLORINDA

Sir, I heartily forgive you all.

BLUNT

That's nobly said, sweet lady. – Belvile, prithee present her her ring again, for I find I have not courage to approach her myself.

Gives him the ring; [BELVILE] *gives it to* FLORINDA

Enter BOY

BOY

Sir, I have brought the Father that you sent for.

BELVILE

'Tis well, and now my dear Florinda, let's fly to complete that mighty joy we have so long wished and sighed for. – Come Fred, you'll follow?

FREDERICK

Your example, sir, 'twas ever my ambition in war, and must be so in love.

WILLMORE

And must not I see this juggling knot tied?

BELVILE

No, thou shalt do us better service and be our guard, lest Don Pedro's sudden return interrupt the ceremony.

WILLMORE

Content – I'll secure this pass.

Exeunt BELVILE, FLORINDA, FREDERICK, *and* VALERIA

Enter BOY

BOY (*To* WILLMORE)

Sir, there's a lady without would speak to you.

WILLMORE

Conduct her in, I dare not quit my post.

BOY [*To* BLUNT]

And sir, your tailor waits you in your chamber.

BLUNT

Some comfort yet: I shall not dance naked at the wedding.

Exeunt BLUNT *and* BOY

183 s.d. 1 *gives it to* Q3, C, C2 (ring he gives to Q1, Q2).

190 *juggling* deceitful.

Enter again the BOY, *conducting in* ANGELLICA, *in a masking habit and a vizard.* WILLMORE *runs to her*

WILLMORE

This can be none but my pretty gipsy. – Oh, I see you can follow as well as fly. Come, confess thyself the most malicious devil in nature; you think you have done my business with Angellica –

ANGELLICA

Stand off, base villain –

She draws a pistol, and holds [*it*] *to his breast*

WILLMORE

Ha, 'tis not she! Who art thou, and what's thy business?

ANGELLICA

One thou hast injured, and who comes to kill thee for't.

WILLMORE

What the devil canst thou mean?

ANGELLICA

By all my hopes to kill thee –

Holds still the pistol to his breast; he going back, she following still

WILLMORE

Prithee, on. What acquaintance? For I know thee not.

ANGELLICA

Behold this face – so lost to thy remembrance!

Pulls off her vizard

And then call all thy sins about thy soul,
And let 'em die with thee.

WILLMORE

Angellica!

ANGELLICA

Yes, traitor,
Does not thy guilty blood run shivering through thy veins?
Hast thou no horror at this sight that tells thee
Thou hast not long to boast thy shameful conquest?

WILLMORE

Faith, no, child; my blood keeps its old ebbs and flows still, and

206 *Prithee, on. What* ed. ('Prithee on, what' Q1, Q2; 'Prithee on what' Q3, C, C2).
211 *traitor* Q2, Q3, C, C2 (tailor Q1).

that usual heat too, that could oblige thee with a kindness, had I but opportunity.

ANGELLICA

Devil! Dost wanton with my pain? – Have at thy heart!

WILLMORE

Hold, dear virago! Hold thy hand a little;
I am not now at leisure to be killed. Hold, and hear me.
(*Aside*) – Death, I think she's in earnest.

ANGELLICA (*Aside, turning from him*)

Oh, if I take not heed,
My coward heart will leave me to his mercy.
– What have you, sir, to say? – But should I hear thee,
Thou'ldst talk away all that is brave about me:

Follows him with the pistol to his breast

And I have vowed thy death by all that's sacred.

WILLMORE

Why then, there's an end of a proper handsome fellow,
That might 'a lived to have done good service yet.
– That's all I can say to't.

ANGELLICA (*Pausingly*)

Yet – I would give thee – time for – penitence.

WILLMORE

Faith, child, I thank God I have ever took care to lead a good, sober, hopeful life, and am of a religion that teaches me to believe I shall depart in peace.

ANGELLICA

So will the devil! Tell me,
How many poor believing fools thou hast undone?
How many hearts thou hast betrayed to ruin?
– Yet these are little mischiefs to the ills
Thou'st taught mine to commit: thou'st taught it love!

WILLMORE

Egad, 'twas shrewdly hurt the while.

ANGELLICA

Love, that has robbed it of its unconcern,
Of all that pride that taught me how to value it.

219 *virago* heroic woman, female warrior.
225 *Thou'ldst* ed. (Thoud'st Q1).
228 *'a* i.e. have Q1, Q2, C (have Q3, C2).
231–3 prose ed. (verse Q1).

And in its room
A mean submissive passion was conveyed,
That made me humbly bow, which I ne'er did
To anything but Heaven.
Thou, perjured man, didst this, and with thy oaths,
Which on thy knees thou didst devoutly make,
Softened my yielding heart – and then, I was a slave.
– Yet still had been content to've worn my chains,
Worn 'em with vanity and joy forever,
Had'st thou not broke those vows that put them on.
'Twas then I was undone.

All this while follows him with the pistol to his breast

WILLMORE
Broke my vows! Why, where hast thou lived?
Amongst the gods? For I never heard of mortal man
That has not broke a thousand vows.

ANGELLICA
Oh, impudence!

WILLMORE
Angellica! That beauty has been too long tempting
Not to have made a thousand lovers languish,
Who, in the amorous fever, no doubt have sworn
Like me. Did they all die in that faith? Still adoring?
I do not think they did.

ANGELLICA
No, faithless man: had I repaid their vows, as I did thine,
I would have killed the ingrateful that had abandoned me.

WILLMORE
This old general has quite spoiled thee. Nothing makes a woman so vain as being flattered; your old lover ever supplies the defects of age with intolerable dotage, vast charge, and that which you call constancy; and attributing all this to your own merits, you domineer, and throw your favours in's teeth, upbraiding him still with the defects of age, and cuckold him as often as he deceives your expectations. But the gay, young, brisk lover, that brings his equal fires, and can give you dart for dart, you'll find will be as nice as you sometimes.

259 *fever* Q3 (favour Q1, Q2, C, C2).
271–2 *you'll find will* emendation (ms note) in Luttrell Q1 ('you'l will be' Q1; 'he'll be' Q2,C,C2 'will be' Q3) *nice* fastidious.

ANGELLICA

All this thou'st made me know, for which I hate thee.
Had I remained in innocent security,
I should have thought all men were born my slaves,
And worn my power like lightning in my eyes,
To have destroyed at pleasure when offended.
But when love held the mirror, the undeceiving glass
Reflected all the weakness of my soul, and made me know
My richest treasure being lost, my honour,
All the remaining spoil could not be worth
The conqueror's care or value.
Oh, how I fell like a long-worshipped idol,
Discovering all the cheat.
Would not the incense and rich sacrifice
Which blind devotion offered at my altars
Have fallen to thee?
Why would'st thou then destroy my fancied power?

WILLMORE

By Heaven, thou'rt brave, and I admire thee strangely.
I wish I were that dull, that constant thing
Which thou would'st have, and nature never meant me.
I must, like cheerful birds, sing in all groves,
And perch on every bough,
Billing the next kind she that flies to meet me.
Yet, after all, could build my nest with thee,
Thither repairing when I'd loved my round,
And still reserve a tributary flame.
– To gain your credit, I'll pay you back your charity,
And be obliged for nothing but for love.

Offers her a purse of gold

ANGELLICA

Oh, that thou wert in earnest!
So mean a thought of me
Would turn my rage to scorn, and I should pity thee,
And give thee leave to live;
Which, for the public safety of our sex,
And my own private injuries, I dare not do.
Prepare –

Follows still as before

I will no more be tempted with replies.

WILLMORE

Sure –

ANGELLICA

Another word will damn thee! I've heard thee talk too long.

She follows him with the pistol ready to shoot; he retires, still amazed. Enter DON ANTONIO, *his arm in a scarf, and lays hold on the pistol*

ANTONIO

Ha! Angellica!

ANGELLICA

Antonio! What devil brought thee hither?

ANTONIO

Love and curiosity, seeing your coach at door. Let me disarm you of this unbecoming instrument of death. – (*Takes away the pistol*) Amongst the number of your slaves, was there not one worthy the honour to have fought your quarrel? [*To* WILLMORE] – Who are you, sir, that are so very wretched to merit death from her?

WILLMORE

One, sir, that could have made a better end of an amorous quarrel without you, than with you.

ANTONIO

Sure, 'tis some rival. – Ha! The very man took down her picture yesterday – the very same that set on me last night. – Blest opportunity!

Offers to shoot him

ANGELLICA

Hold! You're mistaken, sir.

ANTONIO

By Heaven, the very same!
– Sir, what pretensions have you to this lady?

WILLMORE

Sir, I do not use to be examined, and am ill at all disputes but this –

Draws: ANTONIO *offers to shoot*

313–14 s.d. Q3 (s.d. follows Antonio's speech Q1, Q2, C, C2).
320 *took down her picture* See II.i.94 s.d.

ANGELLICA (*To* WILLMORE)
Oh, hold! You see he's armed with certain death.
– And you, Antonio, I command you hold,
By all the passion you've so lately vowed me.

Enter DON PEDRO, *sees* ANTONIO, *and stays*

PEDRO (*Aside*)
Ha, Antonio! And Angellica!

ANTONIO
When I refuse obedience to your will,
May you destroy me with your mortal hate.
By all that's holy, I adore you so,
That even my rival, who has charms enough
To make him fall a victim to my jealousy,
Shall live; nay, and have leave to love on still.

PEDRO (*Aside*)
What's this I hear?

ANGELLICA (*Pointing to* WILLMORE)
Ah, thus! 'Twas thus! He talked, and I believed.
– Antonio, yesterday,
I'd not have sold my interest in his heart
For all the sword has won and lost in battle.
[*To* WILLMORE] – But now, to show my utmost of contempt,
I give thee life – which if thou would'st preserve,
Live where my eyes may never see thee more,
Live to undo someone, whose soul may prove
So bravely constant to revenge my love.

Goes out. ANTONIO *follows, but* PEDRO *pulls him back*

PEDRO
Antonio – stay.

ANTONIO
Don Pedro –

PEDRO
What coward fear was that prevented thee
From meeting me this morning on the Molo?

ANTONIO
Meet thee?

PEDRO
Yes, me. I was the man that dared thee to't.

ANTONIO

Hast thou so often seen me fight in war,
To find no better cause to excuse my absence?
I sent my sword and one to do thee right,
Finding myself incapable to use a sword.

PEDRO

But 'twas Florinda's quarrel that we fought,
And you, to show how little you esteemed her,
Sent me your rival, giving him your interest.
But I have found the cause of this affront,
And when I meet you fit for the dispute,
I'll tell you my resentment.

ANTONIO

I shall be ready, sir, ere long, to do you reason. *Exit*

PEDRO

If I could find Florinda, now, whilst my anger's high, I think I should be kind, and give her to Belvile in revenge.

WILLMORE

Faith, sir, I know not what you would do, but I believe the priest within has been so kind.

PEDRO

How! My sister married?

WILLMORE

I hope by this time she is, and bedded too, or he has not my longings about him.

PEDRO

Dares he do this? Does he not fear my power?

WILLMORE

Faith, not at all; if you will go in and thank him for the favour he has done your sister, so. If not, sir, my power's greater in this house than yours. I have a damned surly crew here that will keep you till the next tide, and then clap you on board for prize. My ship lies but a league off the Molo, and we shall show your donship a damned Tramontana rover's trick.

Enter BELVILE

BELVILE

This rogue's in some new mischief. – Ha, Pedro returned!

357 *incapable* ed. (uncapable Q1).
370 *she* C, C2 (he Q1–3).
378 *Tramontana rover* foreign pirate.

PEDRO
Colonel Belvile, I hear you have married my sister.

BELVILE
You have heard truth then, sir.

PEDRO
Have I so? Then sir, I wish you joy.

BELVILE
How?

PEDRO
By this embrace, I do, and I am glad on't.

BELVILE
Are you in earnest?

PEDRO
By our long friendship and my obligations to thee, I am.
The sudden change, I'll give you reasons for anon.
Come, lead me to my sister,
That she may know I now approve her choice.

Exit BELVILE *with* PEDRO. WILLMORE *goes to follow them. Enter* HELLENA, *as before in boy's clothes, and pulls him back*

WILLMORE
Ha, my gipsy! – Now a thousand blessings on thee for this kindness. Egad, child, I was e'en in despair of ever seeing thee again. My friends are all provided for within, each man his kind woman.

HELLENA
Ha! I thought they had served me some such trick!

WILLMORE
And I was e'en resolved to go abroad, and condemn myself to my lone cabin, and the thoughts of thee.

HELLENA
And could you have left me behind? Would you have been so ill-natured?

WILLMORE
Why, 'twould have broke my heart, child – but since we are met again, I defy foul weather to part us.

HELLENA
And would you be a faithful friend now, if a maid should trust you?

WILLMORE
For a friend, I cannot promise; thou art of a form so excellent,

a face and humour too good for cold, dull friendship. I am parlously afraid of being in love, child, and you have not forgot how severely you have used me?

HELLENA

That's all one; such usage you must still look for – to find out all your haunts, to rail at you to all that love you, till I have made you love only me in your own defence, because nobody else will love you.

WILLMORE

But hast thou no better quality to recommend thyself by?

HELLENA

Faith, none, captain. Why, 'twill be the greater charity to take me for thy mistress. I am a lone child, a kind of orphan lover, and why I should die a maid, and in a captain's hands, too, I do not understand.

WILLMORE

Egad, I was never clawed away with broadsides from any female before. Thou hast one virtue I adore – good nature. I hate a coy, demure mistress; she's as troublesome as a colt. I'll break none. No, give me a mad mistress when mewed, and in flying, one I dare trust upon the wing that whilst she's kind will come to the lure.

HELLENA

Nay, as kind as you will, good captain, whilst it lasts, but let's lose no time.

WILLMORE

My time's as precious to me as thine can be; therefore, dear creature, since we are so well agreed, let's retire to my chamber, and if ever thou wert treated with such savoury love! Come – my bed's prepared for such a guest all clean and sweet as thy fair self. I love to steal a dish and a bottle with a friend, and hate long graces. – Come, let's retire and fall to.

HELLENA

'Tis but getting my consent, and the business is soon done. Let

407 *love you* Q3 (love Q1, Q2, C, C2).
415 *clawed away* scolded, railed at.
broadsides the simultaneous discharge of artillery from one side of a war-ship.
418 *mewed* See III.i.4 note.
flying, one Summers, vol. 1, p. 100 (flying on Q1–3, C, C2).
419–20 *come . . . lure* as a bird of prey flies back to the handler for food.
428 *fall to* C2 (fall too Q1) See III.i.150 note.

but old gaffer Hymen and his priest say amen to't, and I dare lay my mother's daughter by as proper a fellow as your father's son, without fear or blushing.

WILLMORE

Hold, hold, no bug words, child. Priest and Hymen! Prithee add a hang-man to 'em to make up the consort. No, no, we'll have no vows but love, child, nor witness but the lover; the kind deity enjoin naught but love and enjoy! Hymen and priest wait still upon portion and jointure; love and beauty have their own ceremonies. Marriage is as certain a bane to love as lending money is to friendship: I'll neither ask nor give a vow – though I could be content to turn gipsy, and become a left-handed bridegroom, to have the pleasure of working that great miracle of making a maid a mother, if you durst venture. 'Tis upse gipsy that, and if I miss, I'll lose my labour.

HELLENA

And if you do not lose, what shall I get? A cradle full of noise and mischief, with a pack of repentance at my back? Can you teach me to weave incle to pass my time with? 'Tis upse gipsy that, too.

WILLMORE

I can teach thee to weave a true love's knot better.

HELLENA

So can my dog.

WILLMORE

Well, I see we are both upon our guards, and I see there's no way to conquer good nature, but by yielding. Here – give me thy hand – one kiss and I am thine –

HELLENA

One kiss! How like my page he speaks; I am resolved you shall

430 *gaffer* old man.
Hymen god of marriage.
433 *bug words* words meant to frighten or threaten.
434 *consort* company, partnership.
436 *enjoin* ed. (injoin Q1–3; injoins C, C2).
enjoy (injoy Q1).
437 *portion* marriage portion, dowry.
jointure 1) dowry 2) the joint holding of property by husband and wife 3) the agreed provision of lands etc. for the wife, to take effect after the husband's death.
440–1 *left-handed bridegroom* i.e. bridegroom of an illegal or fictitious marriage.
442 *upse gipsy* in the gipsy fashion.
446 *incle* linen thread or yarn from which the tape known as 'incle' was manufactured.

have none for asking such a sneaking sum. He that will be satisfied with one kiss will never die of that longing; good friend single-kiss, is all your talking come to this? A kiss, a caudle! Farewell captain single-kiss.

Going out, he stays her

WILLMORE

Nay, if we part so, let me die like a bird upon a bough, at the sheriff's charge. By Heaven, both the Indies shall not buy thee from me. I adore thy humour and will marry thee, and we are so of one humour, it must be a bargain. – Give me thy hand (*Kisses her hand*) – and now let the blind ones, love and fortune, do their worst.

HELLENA

Why, God-a-mercy captain!

WILLMORE

But hark'ee – the bargain is now made; but is it not fit we should know each other's names, that when we have reason to curse one another hereafter, and people ask me who 'tis I give to the devil, I may at least be able to tell what family you came of?

HELLENA

Good reason, captain; and where I have cause (as I doubt not but I shall have plentiful) that I may know at whom to throw my – blessings. I beseech ye your name.

WILLMORE

I am called Robert the Constant.

HELLENA

A very fine name! Pray was it your falconer or butler that christened you? Do they not use to whistle when they call you?

WILLMORE

I hope you have a better, that a man may name without crossing himself, you are so merry with mine.

HELLENA

I am called Hellena the Inconstant.

457 *caudle* warm drink of thin gruel and wine or ale, given to the sick.

458 *let me . . . bough* i.e. let me be hanged.

462–3 *blind . . . fortune* Both Cupid, god of love, and Fortune were depicted wearing blind-folds.

473 *falconer* keeper of hawks.
butler originally, the servant in charge of the wine-cellar. She may be implying that he is a predatory man, only steadfast in his attachments to prey (i.e. women), and to drink.

Enter PEDRO, BELVILE, FLORINDA, FREDERICK [*and*] VALERIA

PEDRO
Ha! Hellena!

FLORINDA
Hellena!

HELLENA
The very same. Ha, my brother! Now captain, show your love and courage; stand to your arms and defend me bravely, or I am lost forever.

PEDRO
What's this I hear? False girl, how came you hither, and what's your business? Speak.

Goes roughly to her

WILLMORE
Hold off, sir; you have leave to parley only.

Puts himself between

HELLENA
I had e'en as good tell it, as you guess it. Faith, brother, my business is the same with all living creatures of my age: to love and be beloved, and here's the man.

PEDRO
Perfidious maid, hast thou deceived me, too; deceived thyself and Heaven?

HELLENA
'Tis time enough to make my peace with that,
Be you but kind, let me alone with Heaven.

PEDRO
Belvile, I did not expect this false play from you; was't not enough you'd gain Florinda (which I pardoned), but your lewd friends, too, must be enriched with the spoils of a noble family?

BELVILE
Faith, sir, I am as much surprised at this as you can be. Yet, sir, my friends are gentlemen, and ought to be esteemed for their misfortunes, since they have the glory to suffer with the best of men and kings; 'tis true, he's a rover of fortune, yet a prince aboard his little wooden world.

494 *you'd gain* Q1, Q2, C, C2 (you gained Q3).

PEDRO

What's this to the maintenance of a woman of her birth and quality?

WILLMORE

Faith, sir, I can boast of nothing but a sword which does me right where'er I come, and has defended a worse cause than a woman's; and since I loved her before I either knew her birth or name, I must pursue my resolution, and marry her.

PEDRO [*To* HELLENA]

And is all your holy intent of becoming a nun, debauched into a desire of man?

HELLENA

Why, I have considered the matter, brother, and find the two hundred thousand crowns my uncle left me (and you cannot keep from me) will be better laid out in love than in religion, and turn to as good an account. – Let most voices carry it: for Heaven or the captain?

ALL (*Cry*)

A captain! A captain!

HELLENA

Look ye, sir, 'tis a clear case.

PEDRO

Oh, I am mad! (*Aside*) – If I refuse, my life's in danger. – Come, there's one motive induces me. Take her. I shall now be free from fears of her honour; guard it you now, if you can. I have been a slave to't long enough.

Gives her to [WILLMORE]

WILLMORE

Faith, sir, I am of a nation that are of opinion a woman's honour is not worth guarding when she has a mind to part with it.

HELLENA

Well said, captain.

PEDRO (*To* VALERIA)

This was your plot, mistress, but I hope you have married one that will revenge my quarrel to you.

VALERIA

There's no altering destiny, sir.

509 *two* Q3 (three Q1, Q2, C, C2) See IV.ii.184.

PEDRO

Sooner than a woman's will; therefore I forgive you all – and wish you may get my father's pardon as easily; which I fear.

Enter BLUNT, *dressed in a Spanish habit, looking very ridiculously, his* MAN *adjusting his band*

MAN

'Tis very well, sir –

BLUNT

Well, sir! 'Adsheartlikins, I tell you 'tis damnable ill, sir. A Spanish habit! Good Lord! Could the devil and my tailor devise no other punishment for me but the mode of a nation I abominate?

BELVILE

What's the matter, Ned?

BLUNT

Pray view me round, and judge –

Turns round

BELVILE

I must confess thou art a kind of an odd figure.

BLUNT

In a Spanish habit with a vengeance! I had rather be in the Inquisition for Judaism than in this doublet and breeches; a pillory were an easy collar to this three handfuls high; and these shoes, too, are worse than the stocks, with the sole an inch shorter than my foot. In fine, gentlemen, methinks I look altogether like a bag of bays stuffed full of fool's flesh.

BELVILE

Methinks 'tis well, and makes thee look e'en cavalier. Come, sir, settle your face and salute our friends. Lady –

528 s.d. 1 *habit* See I.i.187 note.
s.d. 2 *band* probably his neck band, collar, or waistband. See III.iii.41.

538 *Inquisition for Judaism* Punishments were especially severe in Spain, where the Inquisition had been reorganised by the state and directed against Jews and Moors. *doublet* close-fitting upper garment.

539 *pillory* a wooden frame through which the head and hands of an offender were thrust and exposed to public insult.

540 *stocks* wooden boards locked around an offender's feet with the same purpose as the pillory.

542 *bag of bays* a porous bag of bay leaves and spices used in cooking.

543 *e'en* even.

BLUNT (*To* HELLENA)

Ha! Say'st thou so, my little rover? Lady – if you be one – give me leave to kiss your hand, and tell you, 'adsheartlikins, for all I look so, I am your humble servant. – A pox of my Spanish habit!

WILLMORE

Hark, what's this?

Music is heard to play

Enter BOY

BOY

Sir, as the custom is, the gay people in masquerade, who make every man's house their own, are coming up.

Enter several men and women in masking habits, with music; they put themselves in order and dance

BLUNT

'Adsheartlikins, would 'twere lawful to pull off their false faces, that I might see if my doxy were not amongst 'em.

BELVILE (*To the maskers*)

Ladies and gentlemen, since you are come so *à propos,* you must take a small collation with us.

WILLMORE (*To* HELLENA)

Whilst we'll to the good man within, who stays to give us a cast of his office. Have you no trembling at the near approach?

HELLENA

No more than you have in an engagement or a tempest.

WILLMORE

Egad, thou'rt a brave girl, and I admire thy love and courage.

Lead on, no other dangers they can dread,
Who venture in the storms o'th' marriage bed.

Exeunt

554 s.d. *maskers* Q3, C, C2 (masqueros Q1, Q2).
à propos opportunely.
555 *collation* See III.i.146 note.
556–7 *cast . . . office* i.e. a taste of his office – and, therefore, marriage.
558 *engagement* i.e. in fighting or in battle.

EPILOGUE

The banished cavaliers! A roving blade!
A popish carnival! A masquerade!
The devil's in't if this will please the nation
In these our blessed times of reformation,
When conventickling is so much in fashion.
And yet –
That mutinous tribe less factions do beget,
Than your continual differing in wit.
Your judgement's, as your passion's, a disease:
Nor muse nor miss your appetite can please;
You're grown as nice as queasy consciences,
Whose each convulsion, when the spirit moves,
Damns everything that maggot disapproves.
  With canting rule you would the stage refine,
And to dull method all our sense confine.
With th' insolence of commonwealths you rule,
Where each gay fop and politic grave fool
On monarch wit impose, without control.
As for the last, who seldom sees a play,
Unless it be the old Blackfriars way;
Shaking his empty noddle o'er bamboo,
He cries, 'Good faith, these plays will never do!
Ah, sir, in my young days, what lofty wit,
What high-strained scenes of fighting there were writ.
These are slight airy toys. But tell me, pray,
What has the House of Commons done today?'
Then shows his politics, to let you see
Of state affairs he'll judge as notably
As he can do of wit and poetry.

1 *The banished cavaliers* the play's sub-title.
blade gallant, free and easy fellow.
5 *conventickling* meeting as a non-conformist religious assembly.
7 *That . . . tribe* the dissenters.
13 *maggot* person of perverse fancies.
14 *canting* hypocritical.
20 *Blackfriars* one of the earliest indoor theatres.
21 *o'er bamboo* over a walking stick.

The younger sparks, who hither do resort,
Cry,
'Pox o' your genteel things! Give us more sport!
Damn me, I'm sure 'twill never please the court.'
   Such fops are never pleased, unless the play
Be stuffed with fools as brisk and dull as they.
Such might the half-crown spare, and in a glass
At home behold a more accomplished ass,
Where they may set their cravats, wigs, and faces,
And practise all their buffoon'ry grimaces:
See how this – huff becomes, – this damny, – stare,
Which they at home may act because they dare,
But must with prudent caution do elsewhere.
Oh that our Nokes, or Tony Lee, could show
A fop but half so much to th' life as you.

32 *genteel* Q3 (gentile Q1, Q2; gentle C, C2).
40 *damny* damn me! (expletive).
43 *Nokes . . . Lee* famous contemporary comedians.

POSTSCRIPT

This play had been sooner in print, but for a report about the town (made by some either very malicious or very ignorant) that 'twas *Thomaso* altered; which made the booksellers fear some trouble from the proprietor of that admirable play, which indeed has wit enough to stock a poet, and is not to be pieced or mended by any but the excellent author himself. That I have stolen some hints from it, may be a proof that I valued it more than to pretend to alter it. Had I had the dexterity of some poets, who are not more expert in stealing than in the art of concealing, and who even that way outdo the Spartan boys, I might have appropriated all to myself; but I, vainly proud of my judgement, hang out the sign of Angellica (the only stolen object) to give notice where a great part of the wit dwelt; though if the play of *The Novella* were as well worth remembering as *Thomaso*, they might (bating the name) have as well said I took it from thence. I will only say the plot and business (not to boast on't) is my own; as for the words and characters, I leave the reader to judge and compare 'em with *Thomaso*, to whom I recommend the great entertainment of reading it. Though had this succeeded ill, I should have had no need of imploring that justice from the critics, who are naturally so kind to any that pretend to usurp their dominion, especially of our sex, they would doubtless have given me the whole honour on't. Therefore I will only say in English what the famous Virgil does in Latin: I make verses, and others have the fame.

FINIS

3 *Thomaso Thomaso, or, The Wanderer:* a closet drama by Thomas Killigrew, written in 1654.

8 it. ed. (it, Q1).

10 *boys*, ed. (boys. Q1).

13 *The Novella* Richard Brome's comedy of intrigue (1632).

21 *especially . . . sex* omitted in Q1 first issue and some copies of the second issue